## C. B. COLBY

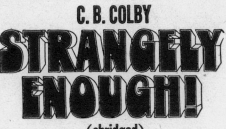

# STRANGELY ENOUGH!

## (abridged)

**Illustrated by David Lockhart**
**Cover Illustrated by Harvey Parks**

This book is sold subject to the condition that it shall not, by way of trade, be lent, re-sold, hired out or otherwise disposed of without the publisher's consent, in any form of binding or cover other than that in which it is published—and without a similar condition, including this condition, being imposed on the subsequent purchaser.

ISBN 0-590-03123-6

Copyright © 1959 by C. B. Colby. Copyright 1954 by Sterling Publishing Co. This edition is published by Scholastic Book Services, a division of Scholastic Magazines, Inc., by arrangement with Sterling Publishing Co.

# SCHOLASTIC BOOK SERVICES
NEW YORK • TORONTO • LONDON • AUCKLAND • SYDNEY • TOKYO

ISBN: 0-590-03123-6

Copyright © 1959 by C. B. Colby. Copyright © 1963 by Scholastic Magazines, Inc. This edition is published by Scholastic Book Services, a division of Scholastic Magazines, Inc., by arrangement with Sterling Publishing Co., Inc.

28 27 26 25 24 23 22 21 .     9/7 0 1 2 3 4/8

Printed in the U.S.A.

# Contents

iv

# ACKNOWLEDGMENTS

It would be impossible for me to name and thank individually all those who have contributed in one way or another to the list of stories on the following pages. Many of the stories came from total strangers I met casually while tracking down others of the list. Some were sent to me anonymously by readers of my column. Others came from long-forgotten diaries, family and town histories. Some were told to me by friends and neighbors who wish to remain nameless.

To all of these people, as well as to the very few ghosts which I have met myself (I think), my deep appreciation. Particular thanks to "the lady in the doorway," whom my daughter Susan and I saw in the Ocean-born Mary house in Henniker, New Hampshire, years ago, for it was she who started my hunt for tales of others of her clan.

The hunt has been a long and exciting one, and often in odd places, but the trophies of the chase on the following pages have made it mighty well worthwhile. I hope you have as much fun reading these stories as I, strangely enough, had tracking them down.

C. B. COLBY

# Introduction

EVERYONE SEEMS TO LIKE a good "off-beat" yarn, a good chilling ghost story, a tale of buried treasure, or perhaps the story of a dream which came true. These and similar stories presented here have been collected over many years, and for them I offer no explanations, if indeed there are any.

A good yarn needs no explanation or excuse for the telling, and these have been selected from those that were particularly popular with the readers of my daily newspaper feature, "Adventure Today." They are presented solely for your entertainment, your wonderment, and your chills. Perhaps you have already encountered a few of them in a local version, or perhaps you are indeed the one to whom "it" happened.

The only ones I can vouch for are those that happened to me personally, and sometimes I wonder even about those. The others are classics of their kind which have been told and retold — and who shall say they never happened? I think it is better to be like the little old lady who said, "I don't believe in ghosts — but I'm afraid of them!" than never to have enjoyed a bit of spine-tingling at the personal encounter with something for which there seems to be no sensible explanation.

As in the case of such things as the "flying saucer," as long as there is a single sighting which cannot be explained in any way, there is that chilling little chance that there might be such things. As long as there are ghosts and supernatural events which cannot be explained away by serious and logical means, we will at least have fine yarns to tell and to hear. May there always be at least one more!

# The Light in the Window

ON A TRAIN GOING THROUGH CANADA one night, some of us were sitting up pretty late telling yarns. One of the chaps in the party told this story:

A friend of his who lived in Ontario became fascinated with an old painting he saw in a dingy little store. The picture was of a castle on a hilltop. The scene was dark and gloomy and every window in the castle was dark except for a small one high in a stone tower. The man wondered why anyone would paint a castle with a light in just one window. Was there a story behind it? He bought the painting and hung it in his home, but all he could learn was that it depicted a castle in Scotland. There was neither signature nor date.

One day, as he was cleaning the painting, he found a few Latin words in a corner. He asked a friend to translate the words for him, and learned that they meant "Every century it will be dark." But this inscription made little sense to either of them, and so it was soon forgotten. The painting hung in the man's home for many years, and his children took pleasure in speculating about why the window was lighted and who had lived up there in the tower. It was quite a source of conversation for many years, but it was to become even more so.

1

One evening the owner of the painting was telling some guests about how he had acquired it and all the questions surrounding its background and meaning. The guests wanted to see this unusual and mysterious piece of art, so they all trooped into the hall where it hung. Imagine their astonishment and the consternation of their host to see that, on the painting, the window in the tower was dark!

They examined the painting and were further astonished to see that the black paint on the once light yellow window was as old and cracked as the paint on the rest of the picture. There were no signs that it had ever been different, let alone bright yellow.

After the guests had gone, the embarrassed host unsuccessfully tried to find a solution to the puzzle. The next morning he returned to the painting and felt his skin crawl — for again the window in the tower was lighted. Then he thought of the Latin inscription, "Every century it will be dark." He made a note of the date and began a serious search into Scottish history. Eventually these facts were uncovered: The castle had been the home of an evil character who had two sons. He hated the elder son and kept him locked in the tower, while his younger son had all the wealth and pleasures he could give him. Exactly five hundred years before the night when the painted window was dark, the imprisoned elder son had died in the little room high in the tower.

# The Lady on the Highway

DRIVING TOWARD MONTGOMERY, ALABAMA, late one night, two businessmen planned to spend the night in a small town on the way. They were making good time through some low country where the road was a few feet above the surrounding land when they spotted a figure far ahead. As they drew nearer they discovered that it was a little old lady walking briskly along the side of the road. In the beam of the headlight, they saw that she wore a pale lavender dress, freshly pressed and sparkling clean. Her hair was neatly done, and as they slowed down to speak to her she turned a smiling face to them. She seemed completely untroubled about walking down a lonely highway in the middle of the night, in an area where snakes and other creatures would make an average woman hesitate to step from a car.

When the men stopped and asked her what she was doing on the road at that time of night, she laughingly explained that she had started out to visit her daughter and grandchildren in Montgomery. She had hoped, she said, to get a ride for at least part of the

3

way, but no one had offered her a lift, so she had just kept on walking.

The two men said they would give her a lift as far as the next town, a two-hour drive, and she was delighted to accept. She sat in the back seat and, as they drove through the night, they talked about her daughter and three grandchildren — their names, where they lived, the children's school — the usual small talk among strangers. When the subject was exhausted, the men eventually became engrossed in business conversation and forgot about the passenger behind them.

When they reached their destination, they stopped to let the elderly lady out. She was gone. Panic-stricken to think that she might have fallen out along the way, they headed back in search of her. But they found no signs of their passenger, even though they retraced their route to where they had picked her up, and saw her tiny footprints in the shoulder of the road where she had first talked to them.

Dismayed and mystified, they drove on to Montgomery to tell her daughter about the accident. After listening to their story in bewilderment, the younger woman pointed to three photos on the mantel. Could they identify their passenger? They did, and she agreed that it was her mother. Without a doubt, they had talked to her. Then they went on to describe her dress, and the woman burst into tears as she said that was the dress her mother had worn when she had last seen her.

"When was that?" they asked her, and she replied between sobs, "When she was buried, just three years ago today!"

4

# The "Seabird"

PHANTOM SHIPS AND VANISHED CREWS have always added to the mystery of the seven seas.

On a strip of land near Newport, Rhode Island, there was a little settlement know as Easton's Beach. Only a few farmers and some fishermen and their families made their homes there.

One day in 1880, a fisherman working on his boat near shore suddenly sighted a full-rigged ship of good size heading straight for land. He thought it very odd that such a large ship under full sail should make no attempt to turn away or head along the coast. But it was coming steadily and directly for shore in the on-shore breeze. He called to the other fishermen nearby and ran to the settlement above the beach to tell the

5

rest of the people about the approaching vessel.

Soon everyone was on the beach, watching in helpless silence as the strange ship came on as though determined to wreck itself, its canvas straining and flags snapping at the mastheads.

With horror the spectators heard the grating of the hull upon the bottom as it struck. Yet the ship still bore down, keeping straight on course as it cut a keel groove in the sandy ocean bottom. When it finally came to rest, it was still on an even keel, with the bowsprit almost over their heads.

Then they recognized the ship. It was the *Seabird*, under the able command of Captain John Husham. It had been to Honduras, and was expected that very day in Newport. Not a sound came from the decks.

At once the crowd went on board to explain the mystery — but it only deepened. Coffee still boiled on the galley stove, food for breakfast was on the table, all navigation instruments and charts were in order. Yet there was no trace of the crew, nor any indication of when, why, or where they had gone. The only living thing aboard the *Seabird* was a mongrel dog shivering on the deck.

The sea had been calm, the breeze fine, and the *Seabird* had been almost exactly on course for Newport. The crew must have left only shortly before the ship appeared on the horizon. But why should they have left the ship when they were so close to their home and families? Only Heaven and a mongrel dog knew what had happened aboard the *Seabird* that sunny morning.

# Preview of Tragedy

PERHAPS YOU HAVE EXPERIENCED strange previews of future events. These premonitions, or coincidences, as you prefer, are often startling and very realistic.

One such alarming glimpse into the future was experienced by the wife of a Swedish industrialist.

One night in 1939, Mrs. Axel Wenner-Gren started up the stairs on her way to bed. It was past midnight, and most of the lights had been extinguished. Only at the landing at the top of the stairs was it still bright. Suddenly a figure appeared before her on the top stair. It was a man, drenched to the skin, as though he had been swimming. In his arms he held the body of a child. Across the child's forehead was a deep cut, which was bleeding.

Mrs. Wenner-Gren screamed, and the figures vanished. Upset and shaken, she described the apparition to her husband. He decided that she was suffering from nerves and suggested that they go off on a trip on their yacht, the *Southern Cross*.

Shortly afterward, on the night of September 3, the yacht went to the aid of the *Athenia*, one of the first ships to be torpedoed in World War II. The very first person to come aboard the yacht was a drenched man, holding out before him the body of a dying child with a deep gash across the forehead. The figures were the ones Mrs. Wenner-Gren had seen at the head of her stairs, at home.

# Witch's Revenge

YEARS AGO, ANY OLD WOMAN who liked to keep to herself and perhaps dressed a little oddly, was soon viewed with fear by those who believed in witches. No matter how harmless and gentle the woman might actually be, she was often said to be endowed with strange powers and the "evil eye." Quite frequently circumstances teamed up with superstition to make such an idea easy to believe.

In New Hampshire, there once lived a family by the name of Emerson. There were two daughters, Sally, the older, and Nabby, the younger. Sally was in love with a young chap, but her parents disapproved of him. They much preferred Stephen Jones, a lazy but well-to-do neighbor in whom Sally had no interest.

One day when the menfolk were to be away, Sally planned to meet her true love, who was about to leave to seek his fortune. She was to decide, this day, if she would join him on his journey. He was forbidden to come to the house, so they had arranged a meeting place.

That morning, after the men had left, an old woman came to the house asking for breakfast. Although this old woman was reputed to be a witch, Sally's mother took no stock in such talk. She told her that they were very busy, but that if she wanted to get her own

8

breakfast she could come in and do so. This angered the woman and she screamed, "Well, mark ye, my fine lady, 'tis little work you'll get done this day before the sun goes down!" And off she went in a rage.

The girls and their mother were astonished at her fury, but laughingly went upstairs to get to their spinning before beginning their other chores. An hour or so later they started down to the kitchen to get to the real work of the day. But the door to the kitchen and street would not open. Its simple latch could be raised easily enough, but, try as they might, the door would not budge. They returned upstairs, opened a window, and called to a passerby who had stopped to water his horse at the trough across the street. He didn't look up.

Again and again they called to people passing by, but no one seemed to hear them, no matter how loudly or long they called. Finally they gave up, and settled down to wait until the men came home to release them.

As the day wore on, they recalled what the old woman had said about their not getting any work done "before the sun goes down." When the sun dipped below the horizon, they again opened the window and called to a neighbor passing below. He looked up at once and then came into the house, opening the door with no trouble at all. He looked at them curiously and left, shaking his head. Their release came too late, for no work had been done that day, and Sally's lover, not finding her at the meeting place, left without her, thinking she had decided to give him up. She married Stephen Jones, as her parents had hoped.

# Daniel Abbott

DANIEL ABBOTT was a lad who lived near Concord, New Hampshire, in the days when the St. Francis Indians were raiding the area. After an attack on his settlement, young Daniel was among a group captured and forced to journey to Canada. The boy had no idea what lay in store for him, but he was spunky and resourceful. From the moment he was taken prisoner, he determined to escape and return home.

In Canada, the frightened captives helped with the squaws' work, but Daniel refused. Instead he entered into the sports of the young Indian boys and repeatedly beat them at their own games. His prowess astonished the Indians, who had looked upon white boys as pretty much a bunch of sissies. Their admiration became so great that they promised to adopt Daniel into their tribe and eventually make him a chieftain.

Although young Abbott was greatly pleased at his

success, he was still determined to escape and secretly resolved to use his high standing to serve that purpose. But the right moment had not arrived, and it was necessary for him to bide his time. Many months passed and he grew both in strength and status.

A raid by the tribe upon a settlement close to the Canadian line finally brought him an unexpected chance at freedom. When the braves returned from the raid, their loot included several pairs of ice skates. They didn't know what they were for, but Daniel told them, and showed them how to put the skates on. On the ice the Indians wobbled and fell, much to their humiliation. Then they insisted that Daniel try them. Although he was an expert skater, he pretended that he was no better than the Indians. Soon the skates were tossed aside as worthless junk.

A short time afterward, when the skates had been forgotten, the boy saw his chance. Unobserved, he fastened a pair securely to his feet and disappeared around a point of the lake shore. By the time the Indians had discovered his ruse, he was far out of reach, even though they shot their arrows after him in anger and frustration at his outwitting them.

Incredible as it may seem, this young man travelled the entire length of Lake Champlain, then followed the rivers and streams as far south as what is now Albany, New York. Finally he reached Concord and his family.

Daniel Abbott in later years became a successful landowner and farmer. He often told the story of his long trip on the captured skates to his 18 children, who all learned to skate at an early age.

# Falling Objects from Heaven

THERE HAVE BEEN a great many accounts of mysterious objects falling from the heavens. Some have been explained eventually, but others never have been.

In my home town, for example, many years ago, there was a sudden rash of falling snowballs from the sky one Sunday morning while almost everyone was in church. A few folks were almost beaned by these freshly packed projectiles from the sky, and my own father had the distinction of solving this short-lived mystery. He was the one to catch me in the belfry.

On the other side of the country, in California, there have been cases of such falling objects which were even more mysterious, and with which I had nothing whatever to do!

At one time, heavy walnuts, small stones, and even small bones were hurled upon a house in Fresno. Even some of the investigating police officers were struck, but no "thrower" was found and the mystery remained unsolved.

Small figures, nails, and bits of broken tile fell into a small printing plant in Los Angeles, near the City Hall. It was reported in a newspaper dated July 2, 1939.

One of the most intriguing and unusual incidents occurred in a section of the little town of Chico, California, in 1922. The objects, which fell in one particular area, consisted of oval rocks of various sizes. Some were tiny things weighing less than an ounce, while others were real dangers weighing nearly a pound. These rocks always fell straight down as though from a great height, and on one day (March 16) they were warm to the touch. The next day a heavy fall of them rained down upon a crowd of curiosity seekers, injuring one of them.

Police checked the entire area around this "target" spot for clues as to where the objects came from, but they found nothing — no person who might have had something to do with them, nor anything else that could account for them. A professor from one of the local colleges joined the investigation and later reported that some of the rocks were of such a size that they could not have been thrown into the area by "ordinary means."

The Chico police marshal, who had seen and heard the stones himself, spent two months trying to solve the mystery, but to no avail. He finally gave up the investigation, yet the stones continued to fall for several more months.

Finally they stopped of their own accord, as though tired of mystifying the residents of Chico. No one has yet been able to explain them.

# The Recovered Painting

ALL SORTS OF LOST OBJECTS TURN UP many years later in strange places. One of the most unusual recoveries was of a painting which later became famous.

George Inness, an American landscape painter during the 19th century, showed great talent at an early age. Long before he attained fame and fortune, he was commissioned by a railroad to paint a picture of its new roundhouse.

For this painting, which was to be used in advertisements, the poor but promising young artist earned the sum of $75. Many copies of the famous ad appeared, and "The Lackawanna Valley" became very well known. The original painting, however, disappeared, and was believed lost or destroyed.

Many years later, when Inness was travelling about the world, he happened to step into a secondhand store in Mexico City. There, before his astonished eyes, was his painting, "The Lackawanna Valley"! How did it get there? Nobody knew. He bought it, and it now hangs in the National Gallery in Washington.

# Battle of the Cheeses

THE SIDE-WHEELER *Arakwe*, built in the closing weeks of the Civil War, was immediately outmoded by the new ironsides and never did get into service. She was assigned a captain and crew, fitted with a couple of small deck-mounted cannons, and given the designation of "gunboat."

At that time the Chilean Government was a bit shaky. To boost morale, the *Arakwe* was sent around the horn to Aconcagua to cruise up and down with her American flag flying and her two small cannons visible. This chore lasted for more than a year and the captain and crew were anxious to return home.

Fortunately, or so the captain thought, the *Arakwe* needed some repairs, so he asked for permission to return to the United States for the work to be done. The letter of permission came, but it arrived just minutes too late.

The mail launch had puffed out to where the *Arakwe* was anchored, and the captain was reading with high elation that his request to return to the United States had been granted when he noticed that his cabin lamp was beginning to swing wildly. He rushed up to the deck and saw, with astonishment, that the waters of the harbor were running out to sea. In a matter of minutes the gunboat would be high and

15

dry. Somewhere there had been a great underwater earthquake, and shortly a tidal wave would rush back into the harbor!

He barked orders to turn the ship, but before it could be swung about she was grounded, stern to the sea. Almost moments later the horrified crew saw a huge tidal wave bearing down upon them from the open sea.

The giant wave crashed over them, sweeping away three men who were never found. The *Arakwe* was swept inland, along with the wreckage of many other ships caught in the catastrophe.

Luckily the *Arakwe's* flat bottom and shallow draft enabled it to stay upright until it crashed into the base of a high cliff two miles inland. The next morning the crew found the area buried under tons of wrecked ships and scattered cargoes, and, like rats running through a dump, hundreds of looting natives were stealing all they could get their hands upon.

16

Eventually these looters turned to the *Arakwe*, and the exhausted sailors had to fight them off in hand-to-hand combat at the tilted rails. Finally, when the looters retired for another attack, the captain ordered that the two small cannons be loaded to repel the mob. But while there was enough powder, the heavy shot was lost in the wrecked hold and could not be reached.

Thinking fast, the captain in desperation ordered all the small round cheeses brought from the galley, and directed them to be loaded into the cannon. Now they were ready.

When the looters charged again, the two cannons roared and down went the attackers in a barrage of cheeses. They didn't make another attempt.

The *Arakwe* never floated again and was broken up where she lay, yet she had fought and won her "Battle of the Cheeses," and is listed in the annals as "lost in action" — a fitting last tribute to a gallant gunboat.

## "Lavender"

DRIVING ALONG A HIGHWAY one evening, two college
boys spotted a very pretty girl in a bright lavender
dress standing by the side of the road. When they
stopped to offer her a lift, she accepted, telling them
that she was going to a dance a couple of miles away.
They, too, were going to a dance, they said. Why
didn't she join them? She agreed, and they talked and
laughed merrily on the way.

At the dance hall she at once became the center of
attention, for in addition to her beauty she was an
excellent dancer and full of bright conversation and
sparkling wit. When asked her name, she laughed and
replied, "Just call me Lavender," and this air of mystery seemed to add to her charms.

18

It was very late when the boys drove her home. The night air had grown cool, and one of her escorts gave her his topcoat to wear. She directed them to her house, a dilapidated shack way back on a rutted dirt road, and the boys bade her good night.

It wasn't until they had arrived at their school that they realized the topcoat had not been returned. The next afternoon, they decided, they would go back for it.

At the shack the next day, a very old woman answered their knock. She knew no "Lavender," she said, and the boys described their companion of the previous evening. Recognition came to her withered face. They had described Lily, she told them, and Lily had been dead for many years. She was buried in an old abandoned cemetery down the road.

The two flustered boys drove away in stunned silence. It was a hoax, they thought, for what other explanation could there be? A few miles down the dirt road they noticed the gravestones of the old cemetery. Impulsively they stopped to look around. There, off to the side, was a small stone with the name "Lily." Neatly folded upon the rounded grave was the missing coat.

# The Coin-filled Boots

THERE IS A HOUSE in Hampton, New Hampshire, that cannot cast off the spell that clings to it. Many persons over the years have insisted that they have seen and heard things in this house that cannot be explained.

It all began when General Jonathan Moulton tried to outsmart the Devil. General Moulton fought bravely in the French and Indian War, and after his military career he returned to the house in Hampton where he was born. There he became wealthy and important, but that was not enough for him. One evening as he was going over his accounts he sighed and declared that he would sell his soul to the very Devil himself if he could become the wealthiest man in the state.

At once a great fountain of sparks burst down—

not up — the chimney and there before him stood the Devil himself. Then and there a bargain was made. In return for the general's soul after death, the Devil agreed to fill his tall boots with golden guineas every month. The general was very pleased with the arrangement and eagerly looked forward to the payments.

Sure enough, on the first of the month the boots were filled with gold, and every month from then on the guineas arrived. Yet even these riches did not satisfy the greedy man. One night, before the money was due, he hung his boots in the usual place in the chimney, but cut the bottoms out of them. When the Devil went to fill them, the coins poured down and out into the room, covering the floor knee-high.

The general was delighted, but soon the Devil realized what was going on. He stopped filling the bottomless boots and, enraged, took back all the gold he had given. Nor did he release the general from his bargain, but turned up to claim his soul when he died.

Ever since then the house was said to be haunted. Noises were heard in empty rooms, and in one room no lamp could be kept going no matter how well it was tended. The lights always went out as though snuffed by an unseen hand.

Many families have lived there since General Moulton's time, but not one stayed long. For years the house stood idle, and then a cobbler rented it, scoffing at the tales he heard. But he too left a short time afterward, for the boots he hung from the rafters in the old house refused to stay there, jumping from the pegs as if they had been pushed by some unseen hand.

# Maximilian's Millions

SOMEWHERE IN TEXAS, near Castle Gap, about fifteen miles east of the Horse Head Crossing of the Pecos River, there lies a treasure estimated to be worth between four and five million dollars.

While the United States was in the midst of the Civil War, Napoleon III of France established the Austrian Archduke Maximilian on the Mexican throne against the wishes of the Mexican people. The new emperor brought with him his personal fortune, and during his precarious stay in Mexico he accumulated still more gold and jewels. However, he was afraid he would never live to enjoy his wealth, and rightly so.

In 1866, a year before he was dethroned and executed, he decided to send his fortune to San Antonio, Texas, for safekeeping. It never got there, and it has never been found.

The treasure was loaded into fifteen oxcarts and guarded by four Austrian friends of the emperor. The fifteen drivers were told that the carts were full of barrels of flour, and they set out for the border and safety. Once across the border, they met six ex-Confederate soldiers who told them the route to San Antonio was beset with hostile Indians and highwaymen. The soldiers were hired to go with them as guards.

One night the soldiers discovered that the "flour"

was treasure and decided that they would get it for themselves. The next night, near Castle Gap, they murdered the Austrians and the Mexican drivers. Then they buried the treasure with the bodies over it and burned the carts. Charred embers were the only visible remains when the six murderers set out for Antonio to spend the money they took with them and to get help to bring in the rest of the huge fortune.

On the way, one of the men became sick and stopped to rest, urging the others to go ahead without him. They believed that he was faking and planned to get more of the treasure for himself, so they shot him and left him for dead.

But the wounded man was not dead, and in a day or so he was able to hobble on after his would-be murderers. Shortly thereafter, he came upon the bodies of the five, who in turn had been murdered and robbed. He kept on and stopped at a camp of horse thieves for the night.

That very night the thieves were captured by a sheriff's posse and the wounded man was thrown into jail with the others. Later he was set free, but a doctor told him he would soon die of blood poisoning. In his last moments he drew a crude map showing where the treasure was buried, and gave it to the doctor.

After the renegades and Indians had been driven from the area, the doctor tried to follow the map to the spot where the carts were burned. He was unable to find it. Somewhere under a sand-covered charcoal heap lies the vast treasure guarded by the bones of nineteen men who never reached their goal, but were revenged by circumstances.

# Lost TV Signal

DID YOU EVER WONDER what becomes of old radio and
TV programs that are sent out into space 24 hours a
day? Do they just fade out and vanish, or do they
keep travelling through space forever, perhaps to be
picked up by creatures on other planets?

Possibly some of the weird sounds that we hear
are really programs (or commercials) from other
planets. It's true that scientific listening posts have put
on tape some mighty odd sounds from space which
might be from some sort of intelligence somewhere.
Some make no sense at all (perhaps those are the
commercials).

In the early days of television some sets retained a
picture long after the program was over. Even today
words from a commercial linger after the advertisement has left the screen, and occasionally another
channel's picture will appear for a few seconds. But
what about pictures that mysteriously appear long
after the program has finished?

In September, 1953, many television screens in England suddenly carried the identification card and call
letters of TV station KLEE in Houston, Texas, thousands of miles across the Atlantic. The image stayed
on the screen long enough for several viewers to take
pictures of the remarkable occurrence. TV usually

fades out after about 150 miles unless helped along with electronic devices and relay stations. In 1953 this was not possible. Even today transatlantic programming is just beginning.

What really startled the TV world was the fact that when the British broadcasting engineers contacted KLEE in Houston to tell them of the unusual event, they learned that the station had been off the air for three years. Since that time no KLEE identification card had been shown.

Where had the picture been for three years? Why did it only appear in England, and how did it get back from wherever it had been?

# Phantom Schooner

PROBABLY ALL OF US, at one time or other, have encountered something that was hard to explain. It might be the feeling of being followed or watched or the hearing of mysterious sounds in the night. It might be a vision of something that wasn't there at all. This is a story of a "something" which apparently wasn't there, even though more than one person was sure that it was. The time was some years ago, the place, the Caribbean, where I was on a patrol cruiser trying to apprehend some smugglers.

The little cruiser was hidden in a tiny palm-ringed cove one night, awaiting the appearance of a certain small schooner known to be in operation in the area. The only light came from the stars and a blinker buoy at sea beyond the entrance to the cove. The moon was down, but by the light of the stars we could distinguish between sea and sky and shore line. We watched and waited.

An hour or so past midnight, one of the crew spotted the dark sails of a small sailboat appearing above the beach by the cove entrance. Soon the silhouette of the little boat, silent and dark, passed in front of us, blotted out the blinking light from the buoy and disappeared behind the point of land to the right of the cove. It might be our quarry.

We pulled up the anchor, started the engines, and moved silently out of the cove, turning south along the coast and keeping close to shore. Ahead of us, also close to shore, we could faintly see the outline of the schooner beating along under a stiff onshore breeze.

As we gained upon the boat ahead we prepared for what might be more than just routine checking of a vessel without legal lights. A belt of ammunition was fed into the machine gun on our bow, sidearms and rifles were passed up from the gunlockers below, and the spray jacket was removed from the big searchlight atop the cabin roof.

Our procedure in such a contact was to come up a bit to the windward and astern of any such boat, snap on the powerful beam, and then close in for whatever action was required, depending upon what the glare of the searchlight revealed. A small schooner without running lights beating close to shore late at night could mean most anything: a careless skipper with a fine disregard for regulations, a forgetful native crew coming home from a celebration in one of the small villages — or it might be the schooner we were after.

We drew close astern of the silhouetted schooner, swung to windward of it so that our boat would cut the wind and slow the boat ahead, and snapped on our big beam. There was absolutely nothing there!

We swung our huge beam around the area, even up and down, but our quarry had vanished. What had we seen, or what had we thought we had seen?

# Bandit's Buried Loot

Monterrey, Mexico, has been the scene of much lawlessness over the years. It was there that an interesting story began one day in 1885, when five bandits held up and robbed a bank. They escaped with about $18,000. Pursued by the *Rurales*, the local law officers, the bandits fled northward across the border into Texas. During the chase, four of the bandits were killed, but one escaped with the loot — all in gold coins.

When he neared old Fort Belknap, he feared that he would be stopped and questioned by the soldiers stationed there. So he hid out for a few days until he saw his chance to steal a cast-iron bean pot from a farmer's house. He put the coins into this pot and buried it, expecting to come back for it later when the excitement had died down.

Not long after, he fell in with a group of renegades. In the course of an argument, they shot him and then rode off, leaving him for dead. Two Texans heard the shots, came to investigate, and found him bleeding to death and nearly unconscious. But before he died, he told them about the buried loot and said they could have it in payment for trying to help him. With his last breath he gave directions: "One mile from Fort Belknap, 256 steps north of a creek, and 86 steps west of a prickly pear tree. It is buried and marked with a swallow fork (stick) and it is buried the depth of a wagon rod with one half the ring showing above ground and three rocks piled against the ring."

The two Texans were pretty skeptical of the bandit's story, but some time later one of them, a man named Carter, decided to see if he could find the location mentioned in the rather garbled directions of the dying man. He retraced the steps of the bandit and finally spotted three stones which seemed to be piled over something. As he began to kick away the stones, he heard a rider coming. It was the owner of the property. Rather than share the treasure with him, Carter said nothing about why he was there and was ordered to leave at once.

Several times later he returned to recover the treasure, but as time passed, dust had covered the half-ring of the wagon rod, the stones all looked alike and the forked stick could not be found. Had nature cheated him out of a fortune, or had the owner become curious himself and discovered the ring and then the treasure? Carter never dared to ask questions for fear he would tip his hand, but unless the owner found and recovered the "pot of gold," it's still there waiting for some lucky person's rainbow to point the way.

# New England's Darkest Day

ALL OF US have known "dark days," but one of the most unusual dark days happened back in the spring of 1780 — on May 19, to be exact.

You can find references to it in many New England town histories that go back that far, and in old books on unusual physical happenings. It has never been completely explained, although there was probably some scientific and sensible explanation for it. The facts alone, however, are intriguing. You can imagine the terror of the citizens — they had no radios or other means of contacting the outside world to find out just how far the darkness had spread.

May 19th dawned as bright and clear as usual, except that there appeared to be a haze to the southwest. (One town history reports that it was raining.) This haze grew darker, and soon the whole sky was covered with a thick cloud which was travelling northeast rapidly. It reached the Canadian border by midmorning. Meanwhile the eastern part of New York as well as Maine, New Hampshire, Rhode Island,

Massachusetts, and Connecticut were becoming darker.

By one o'clock some sections were so dark that white paper held a few inches from the eyes couldn't be seen. It was as dark as a starless night. Apprehension soon turned to panic. Schools were dismissed, and lanterns and candles were lighted in homes and along the streets. One New Hampshire town history reports that chickens and birds went to roost, and that everything "appeared through a kind of Egyptian darkness" — whatever an Egyptian darkness might be!

Many people gathered in churches to pray and await what they assumed was the Judgment Day. However, in one city at least business went on as usual, thanks to a rugged individual. In Hartford, Connecticut, the state legislature was in session. By noon the members were unable even to see each other. The meeting threatened to break up completely in panic, but one of the members arose and addressed the Speaker: "Mr. Speaker, this is either the Day of Judgment, or it is not. If it is not, there is no need for adjourning. If it is, I desire to be found doing my duty. I move that candles be brought in, and that we proceed to business." And so the session continued, with only a few leaving for home in fear and trembling.

That night the darkness continued, and it was noted that by the light of lanterns everything seemed to have a faint greenish hue. A full moon, due to rise at nine, did not show until after 1 A.M., when it appeared high in the sky and blood-red. Shortly afterward stars began to appear, and the following morning the sun was as bright as ever, after 14 hours of the strangest darkness ever to panic staunch New Englanders.

31

# The Sporting Sea Gull

A DOCTOR FRIEND of one of my readers is a man who likes to play golf. He was once vacationing in Maine, and had a chance to play in a foursome at a South Bristol golf course with some friends.

It was a warm day, and the golfers were refreshed by the cool ocean breeze. When they reached the second hole, the doctor got off a good first stroke, and then a corker of a second stroke, dropping his ball close enough to the pin for a probable birdie. It looked like a lucky day for him, and he was a pretty happy golfer as he strode confidently toward the green where his ball had dropped.

Just as he arrived at the green, a sea gull swooped

down, scooped up his ball, and started to take off for parts unknown. Whether the good doctor yelled loud enough to scare the gull, or the bird just decided he'd made a very bad choice of lunch is not sure, but he dropped the ball — but not until he was some yards from the green — a full pitch-shot from the pin. To add to the insult, the rest of the foursome insisted that the doctor play it from there, rules or no rules.

On the next hole the gull was back again. The doctor's tee-shot on the 240-yard third hole hooked into the rough, and it looked as though this was not going to be one of his good days after all. The other three players were most sympathetic about his shot into the rough, but the gull proved to be a good sport, too. It swooped down for a second time and scooped up the ball, starting off as before until it apparently realized that this was not quite sporting.

Again it dropped the ball. But this time it landed on the green, about 10 feet from the pin. The doctor got his birdie (the golfing kind) and the gull left for good, perhaps thinking he'd got in enough golf for one day.

# Antique Saucer

FLYING SAUCERS, or "UFO's" — Unidentified Flying Objects — are nothing new. They have been mentioned for hundreds of years in legends, tribal folklore, and even in print. Years ago, of course, "flying saucers" were not known by that name. They were called "wheels," "ships," "things," and assorted other descriptive names.

One of the most unusual and best-documented "things" seen flying over the United States first appeared on November 22, 1896.

It began one evening in San Francisco, when thousands of folks going home from work spotted a large, dark "cigar-shaped object with stubby wings" travelling northwest across Oakland.

Within a few hours reports began to come in from cities to the north. From Santa Rosa, Sacramento, Chico, and a place called Red Bluff, thousands of people reported seeing the same thing. They did not call it an aircraft or flying machine, for remember this was before the first plane was built. They usually just referred to it as the "thing," the "flying ship," or the "shape."

A little over a week later it returned, moving steadily against the wind. This confounded those who had insisted that it was a balloon. The next four months were full of sightings of the strange object. It was reported in Iowa, Nebraska, Missouri, Wisconsin, and Minnesota in April, and on April 10 it was over Chicago. Thousands of people saw and reported the huge cigar-shaped mystery in the skies. It wasn't until April 20, 1897, that it was no longer reported.

Those who did not see it screamed "fake," while those who swore to its existence frequently came to blows over this slur to their integrity. Even Thomas Edison refused to have anything to do with it. Interviewed by a reporter from the *New York Herald*, he said, "I prefer to devote my time to objects of commercial value." Referring to "airships," Edison said, "At best, airships would be only toys."

We will probably never know what this mysterious thing really was, unless some little green man hops out of a modern saucer, takes a look around, and says in whatever language little green men speak: "Yup, it looks just about as my grandpappy said it did back in 1896!"

# Cigar in the Sky

On November 17, 1882, the strange object illustrated here was seen by E. W. Maunder, a famous astronomer, at the Royal Observatory in Greenwich, England. It was observed not only by Maunder, but by several of his expert colleagues at the observatory. This, remember, was long before "flying saucers" were even thought of, before radar or other electronic detection devices were even dreamed of.

The fantastic shape was spotted quite suddenly as though it had appeared out of nowhere. It moved steadily across the sky while the Royal Observatory experts watched it through a large telescope. Maunder and his associates had time to compare notes, jot down their impressions, and later check them against each other's. They all had seen the same thing.

Although the descriptions varied in wording, they were all basically alike. Whether the shape was described as a "cigar," "torpedo," "spindle," or "shuttle," each observer saw the same silhouette. Had it happened 50 years later, the word used might have been "zeppelin," but such airships were unknown in 1882.

All the witnesses agreed that what they saw was "too fast for a cloud and too slow for a meteor," and that it appeared to be a "definite body with a dark nucleus." It was "extraordinary and alarming."

Perhaps someday we'll know all about these mysterious "UFO's" which every so often are either spotted by eye or observed wandering silently across a radar screen.

# Yonkers Saucer

ONE APRIL, not too long ago, a resident of Yonkers, New York, was using his new high-powered telescope. He was looking in a southwesterly direction, roughly toward New York City. The moon had risen but was not yet in view, being behind him and the house. Suddenly he spotted a fuzzy bright object in line with his view and hastily focused upon it. His first thought was that it was Saturn, rings and all. Then he realized that this instrument was not powerful enough to see Saturn, even if it had been in that location.

The object was about the size of a dime at arm's

length, milky white in color, and tilted slightly (as indicated in the sketch). From the underside (away from the observer) a very faint blue halo was visible. The telescope view showed that the object was moving slowly, was clear-cut and uncluttered with "windows," gadgets, or lights. The only thing to be seen was the sharp outline, a dark line at the base of the "turret," and the faint glow from the underside. He called his wife and a few neighbors, and they watched the object for a full half hour until it vanished behind buildings.

Two nights later, he again spotted it. But it was higher in the sky, smaller, and tilted at a sharper angle. This time nine persons watched it, and it was in view for over a half hour. It still had the same milky-white color, the sharp clear image, and the faint bluish glow from the underside.

The puzzled observer checked with the Hayden Planetarium, and learned that Saturn could not possibly have been seen either from that direction or with that particular telescope. The suggestion was made that it might have been a reflection from the moon. But when the planetarium expert was told that the moon had been hidden behind the house at the time of the sighting, he said, "I'm afraid I can't help you in this matter."

Shortly after this incident, it was reported that a young boy had told his mother about the strange sight he had viewed from his window, which faced New York City. He described a "funny, round airplane, white and with a blue light under it." This surely wasn't Saturn, for the child had no telescope.

# Ghosts That Followed a Ship

THE SEA IS FULL OF MYSTERY, and its history is full of tales of the unusual. Here is a fairly modern ghost story of the deep that has never been solved.

In January of 1925, an oil tanker was plowing through the Pacific toward the Panama Canal when tragedy struck. Two men were overcome by gas while cleaning out an empty cargo hatch and were buried at sea.

Several days later a group of greatly disturbed crewmen approached the captain with an astonishing story. They told him that they had seen both the dead seamen following the ship at twilight the past few nights. The captain refused to take their story seriously, but the reports persisted, and even some of the officers of the ship saw the men.

The heads of the two men would appear in the water off the side of the ship from which they had been buried and seem to follow the ship for a few moments. Then they would vanish again. Since so many men and officers saw the apparitions at the same time, the captain finally decided to bring the matter to the attention of the officials of the company when they docked in New Orleans. They too listened, at first with disbelief, and then with wonder.

One of the company officers suggested that the first mate obtain a camera and be ready for the next appearance of the two ghostly faces in the waves. This was done. Then the officer gave the captain a fresh roll of film, with orders to keep it sealed in his own possession until he had a chance to use it. This the captain promised to do.

Back through the Canal went the tanker, and out again into the Pacific. As the ship reached the same spot in the ocean, once more the two faces appeared alongside at twilight.

The captain broke open the film and loaded the camera himself. When the ghosts next appeared he took six photos, then locked up the camera for safe-keeping and away from any possible tampering.

When they reached port, the film was taken to a commercial photographer for developing and printing. This man knew nothing about the mystery, nor the reason for the photographs which he processed.

Five of the negatives showed nothing unusual, just waves and spray, but the sixth showed what appeared to be the outlines of two heads and faces in the waves. This was enlarged so that they showed up plainly, and it was revealed that the two objects were in the same relation to the ship as the two ghosts reportedly seen by the crewmen and ship's officers.

These interesting photos eventually were inspected by Dr. Hereward Carrington, a noted investigator of psychic phenomena. He checked the story with company officials, and, after looking at the photo, said that there could be no doubt that at least one of the faces in the waves was a realistic photo of the dead man.

Strange things follow the sea, and not all men go down to the sea in ships. Some wear shrouds.

# The Tiger Trainer

CHARLES AND SUSAN, friends of mine, were very happy when they moved into a lovely home they had rented in Carmel, New York. Susan was especially pleased, for she could see her husband off to his New York office every morning and then attend to her chores.

One afternoon, while sewing in her room, she became aware that someone was standing in the doorway looking at her. Thinking her husband had come home early, she continued her work. But when she glanced at the doorway, she saw a tall, dark-haired stranger dressed in a white belted tunic and full white trousers tucked into high black boots. For a few moments they stared at each other. Then, with an arrogant walk, the figure strode across the room and vanished. Somehow, the young woman was not frightened. Fascinated, she remained seated and made a mental note of what she had seen, including the details of the strange figure's costume. That night when her husband returned she told him about it, and they laughed about the weird event.

About two weeks later, while hanging curtains in her living room, Susan felt a sudden desire to sing an unfamiliar song she had never heard before. She sang for several minutes — not as herself, but as a sort of "loudspeaker" for someone who was not actually present. Later when the urge had passed, she jotted down the lyrics and again told her husband about this second mysterious event.

Shortly thereafter, she read an advertisement for a small apartment in the local paper. Although she had no need for an apartment, she had an uncontrollable urge to investigate. To her husband's cheerful disgust, she telephoned the man who had placed the ad. After speaking with him for a few moments, she discovered that they had friends in common, so she accepted his invitation to come by with her husband that evening for a chat.

When the two entered this man's home, they both had the strange desire to buy it, and mentioned their feeling to their host. The owner of the house seemed startled, but said that perhaps they could make the purchase, for he had just put it on the market the day before.

Investigating the property, they found that it had originally belonged to a famous menagerie owner and tiger trainer, James Raymond. The house had been moved a few yards from its original site. Raymond used the garage to house his tigers, and the interior walls still bore such warnings as "Beware of Wild Animals." The young couple also found that Raymond had been fond of Stephen Foster songs. It didn't take Susan long to realize that the song she was "forced" to sing was a little-known Foster song.

They soon bought the place, and one evening Charles laughingly said, "I wonder what a tiger trainer of that period wore in the ring?" Without hesitation Susan replied, "Why, a sort of white tunic with a sash, Cossack pants, and black boots!" The two stared at each other, and Charles, with some trepidation, looked up at the ceiling and remarked, "Well, if James Raymond got us to buy this place, perhaps he'll give us a sign that he approves of the deal." The next day he did.

While Susan was sewing upstairs, she heard a noise below and looked down into the living room. A locked door, which she had never opened, suddenly gave the "sign." While she watched, the handle slowly turned and the door swung open. It remained that way until she closed it. Had James Reynolds come back home?

# The Painting in the Cavern

FROM THE WINDOW of my room in Puerto Rico I could see the battlements and moats of San Cristobal, the famous old Spanish fort. Many times I explored its underground tunnels alive with giant insects, climbed over its battlements, and visited the famous haunted sentry box down by the crumbling sea wall. There was one part of the fort I had never been to: the great underground cisterns for drinking water. I had heard they were so huge that a rowboat was needed

45

to get about from one to another. There is a strange tale about the San Cristobal cisterns.

A local resident, the story goes, had persuaded a friend to visit these gloomy, dripping, and altogether unpleasant underground "lakes" to see what they were like. They obtained an old boat, some oars, and a lantern, and, after considerable trouble getting the boat down through the tunnels, they launched it upon the now stagnant waters of the stone reservoirs deep within the vast walls of San Cristobal.

In one of the gloomy water-filled rooms the light of their lantern fell upon an oil painting hanging on a wall. They rowed closer, and saw that it was a lovely painting of some religious scene. It was a shame to leave such a beautiful picture there unseen by anyone, they decided, so with great difficulty they removed it and took it to the local man's home. His wife objected, for who knew what germs it carried or who its owner was? But, over her protests, the painting was hung on a wide stairway wall.

The next morning, the wife saw that it was gone and thought her husband had relented and taken it back. He, in turn, thought she had removed it. For days neither spoke of its disappearance, until the friend who had helped bring it there asked what had happened to it after all their hard work. The man and wife both confessed they had not touched it.

Mystified, the men returned to the underground cistern with the boat, and sure enough, the painting was once more back on the wall deep below the ground. This time they did not touch it, and it may very well be there still.

# Phantom Brig

On July 11, 1881, Prince George of Wales, who became King George V of England, was sailing with his brother Prince Albert Victor on Her Majesty's ship *Inconstant*. They were en route from Melbourne to Sydney, Australia.

As the ship plowed along through the calm water at about four o'clock in the morning, an eerie red light appeared off the port bow. It grew larger and larger until the attention of the men on deck was directed to it. The red glow continued to increase in size and, as it did so, the watchers were aware that in its center was the silhouette of a ship — a brig.

The silhouette grew larger until the spars, masts, sails and rigging were clearly visible. The ship appeared to be no more than a couple of hundred yards away, heading almost directly for the *Inconstant*. The lookout in the forecastle reported the ship as being close to the port bow, while the officer of the watch on the bridge also saw her clearly.

In all, thirteen persons saw the ship's silhouette in the center of the red glow. Two other ships of the squadron, *H.M.S. Tourmaline* and *H.M.S. Cleopatra*, sailing on the opposite side of the red light, also reported it.

The quarterdeck midshipman on the *Inconstant,* one of the men who saw it, was ordered forward to the forecastle; but when he arrived, the glow and the brig had completely faded away. There was no longer any sign of a ship or any unusual light.

The Prince's diary included details of the phantom ship. There have been many tales of strange sights at sea, but how often is a future king a witness?

# Trap-gun Mystery

NEAR KINGMAN, ARIZONA, some men were clearing the land for firewood when they came across a tree that seemed most peculiar. It was a cottonwood tree in which they saw something protruding from both sides of the trunk, 30 feet up. From the distance the men could not tell what it was. They guessed that it might be a piece of piping or perhaps an old pioneer tool.

When the tree was cut down, they discovered that it was all the metal parts of a very early Winchester rifle. This old lever-action rifle was completely covered except for about six inches of the muzzle end of the barrel and the rear portion of the metal action. The stock had long since rotted away and was gone. The hammer of the rifle was down, so they knew that it had been fired. Along with the rifle, there were bits of chicken wire embedded in the trunk of the tree.

The men knew that during the late 19th century there had been much gold-mining activity in that part of Arizona. This fact, along with what they had found, seemed to add up to what was known to have been a trick of the old miners — the setting of a trap gun to protect the cabin while they were away. The miners would put a rifle in a tree crotch and wire it securely with chicken wire so that it was aimed at the cabin door. Then a second wire was rigged, so that if anyone

49

tampered with the door during their absence, he would receive a blast of fire from the hidden rifle.

However, there were certain mysterious angles which no one has ever completely solved. For example, why should anyone have abandoned a perfectly good rifle to the elements? Why was this rifle never removed from the tree after it was fired?

Could it be that the owner of the mine and the cabin had come home, perhaps after too much celebrating, and been killed by his own gun? Or had he been killed in some other accident, only to have his rifle shoot a visiting bear who tried to enter the abandoned cabin? Any way you look at it, the mystery of the fired but abandoned old Winchester only becomes more involved.

This section of the tree trunk with the weapon still embedded in it is now on display at the Mohave Tourist Center and Museum, where Highways 66 and 93 meet in Kingman, Arizona. Perhaps you can solve the mystery of this puzzling relic of a hectic time in our country's history.

# Lost Inca Treasure

THE INCAS, who lived in Mexico and South America, were known for their fabulous treasures of gold. The gold was so plentiful that these skilled Indians not only adorned their temples and shrines with it, but made all their household articles from this costly metal. They say that in the year 1730 alone, the Mexican mines produced over 50 million dollars worth of gold

When Pizarro invaded the Inca territory, he captured the Emperor Atahualpa and held him for ransom. In payment for their leader's release, the Incas led 11,000 treasure-laden llamas through the mountains of Peru. Deep in the mountains, while en route to the appointed spot, the bearers received word by runner that Pizarro had treacherously assassinated Emperor Atahualpa in spite of the fact that the vast ransom was on its way. The angry and sorrowful Incas felt there was no need to continue the trip any longer.

Realizing that Pizarro would still seek out the treasure, it was unloaded from the backs of the shaggy beasts and hidden away in the many caves and valleys of the mountains. The gold was concealed so cleverly, and the secret of its hiding place was so well kept, that to this day the enormous fortune is still one of the few really great missing treasures of the world.

A few trinkets of pure gold, a statue studded with jewels, and three solid gold coffins which have turned up, help keep alive the story of the vast missing hoard of treasure. Somewhere, deep in the mountains of Peru, this enormous hoard still lies waiting for some lucky searcher to find it.

# R-101 Mystery

ALTHOUGH NOT MANY OF US take stories of ghosts, psychic phenomena, spirit rapping, and table tipping seriously, such tales do arouse our interest and curiosity. This story, which *perhaps* explains a great air tragedy, can shake our skepticism.

It occurred in 1930 when Harry Price, a famous psychical researcher who delighted in exposing haunted houses, fake mediums, and assorted would-be mysteries, made an appointment with Eileen Garrett. Mrs. Garrett, a psychic, had been able to go into trances, during which she made startling statements even she could not explain.

Two days before she and Mr. Price were to meet, the world was shocked by the tragic crash of the great British dirigible R-101. This great, lighter-than-air craft crashed, exploded, and burned on the morning of October 5, in open country, near the city of Beauvais, France. Forty-five of her crew were killed. Flight Lieutenant H. C. Irwin, commander of the craft, lost his life in the tragedy.

Mrs. Garrett knew nothing whatever about aviation or aerodynamics or flying. Her interest in the crash was no greater than any other outsider's. But, when she went into a trance in Mr. Price's laboratory two days later, a strange thing took place.

Her voice changed, and, in the excited and condemning voice of a man who identified himself as Flight Lieutenant Irwin, she began to tell what had caused the tragedy. She used technical terms that only an aviation expert would know. Mrs. Garrett, in Lieutenant Irwin's voice, said: "Useful lift too small; elevator jammed; gross lift computed badly; hulk of dirigible too much for her engine capacity; we almost scraped the roofs of Achy. This exorbitant scheme of carbon and hydrogen is absolutely wrong!"

Mr. Price was completely baffled. So was Mrs. Garrett when she came out of the trance. Since the town of Achy had not appeared in any report of the air tragedy, the words seemed completely unconnected with the crash.

Shortly thereafter, there was a new development. The officials of the tiny town of Achy, which *had* been on the flight map used by Commander Irwin, sent in an astonishing report. The great aircraft had flown so low over the roofs that it had almost scraped the church tower.

Furthermore, final reports on the cause of the crash proved the complete truth of the words spoken in the trance, even to the statement about the "scheme of carbon and hydrogen," which had been a closely guarded military secret! Lieutenant Irwin had been one of the very few who knew about it.

54

# The Doomed Sentry

SAN CRISTOBAL harbors another mystery — that of the haunted sentry box.

There are many sentry boxes there, sticking out like thumbs. Some have fancy ball tops and others have none, for they were probably knocked off over the years. The sentry boxes are entered through narrow passages between the walls. From the slit windows the lonely sentry can observe the sea and other approaches.

There is one sentry box that has a weird story. It is below the main part of the fortress and can be seen by looking down over one of the walls high above it. The coast runs west beyond it and the gray bulk of Morro Castle, another fortress guarding the entrance to San Juan Harbor, looms in the distance.

According to the legend, many years ago a sentry was sent to this box to keep watch out to sea. It was a lonely post and none of the garrison wanted the job, but the man chosen could not disobey orders, and off he went, in spite of a premonition that he would not return. He even mentioned his apprehension to some of his buddies, but they merely laughed it off.

Some hours later another soldier was sent to relieve him at his post. The sentry box was empty. There was only a queer pungent smell that filled the lonely stone structure down by the water. What happened to the sentry? Perhaps he had run away, or had fallen into the water from the narrow walk between the low approach walls. There was no trace of him. Even his weapons had vanished.

This disappearance was reported to his superiors, who suspected that the soldier had deserted. From a high point on the fortress walls above, an officer watched the box and the new sentry on duty.

For some hours all was quiet in the box below the wall. Then, suddenly, the officer heard a piercing scream ring out above the roar of the surf. He sprang to his feet for a better look, and saw a bright light coming from inside the tiny stone box.

The light grew brighter and brighter until he could no longer look at it, and then it faded away as a huge black cloud of smoke issued from the gun ports and doorway and drifted out to sea. Then all was quiet.

The officer gathered together a band of men, and they hurried down the slope to the open stone door. Inside there was silence, for there was no one there. No trace of the second soldier remained, but the inside of the box was black with soot and a strong odor of sulphur and brimstone was thick about the gray walls. The men fled back to the fortress above, and the haunted sentry box was never used again.

# Fireballs

Captain Harry White is one of the few men who have actually seen an unexplained "UFO." He has also seen such aerial oddities as fireballs ahead of his plane during electrical storms, when the air and his plane were heavily charged with static electricity. His description of their formation and eventual explosion is the subject of the illustration.

All transport aircraft are equipped with static discharging equipment which looks like small tufted rods extending backward from the outer panels of the main wings. From these, charges of electricity stream off into the air, keeping the craft relatively free of them. Occasionally they build up too rapidly for an adequate discharge. Under certain conditions, this electricity accumulates about the nose of the craft, producing an unusual display of celestial fireworks — a fireball.

According to Captain White, he first began to notice faint veins of light running across the windshields and perhaps along the nose of the giant transport, ahead of the windshield. Next he realized that in front of that nose a small ball of light was bouncing along in the air, keeping just a few feet ahead of the plane. It gradually grew larger and larger until it was about the size of a big basketball. Captain White used to watch these fireballs grow, but not any longer.

The first time he witnessed this astonishing phenomenon, he continued to watch the ball grow larger. Now that he knows better, the moment such a static fireball appears, he and his co-pilot duck down below the windshield, for it will soon explode in a blinding flash of light right before their eyes.

Although the exploding fireball does not endanger the plane or its occupants, it can momentarily blind whoever watches it burst into its fiery end. The static from such a buildup is so great that it makes use of the radio almost impossible. While the explosion of the ball is drowned out by the noise of the plane's engines, the flash alone is enough to startle even the most experienced pilots and their crews.

# The Ghost in the Graveyard

GOING HOME LATE ONE DARK NIGHT, a local resident of the upper New York State area decided to take a short cut through the small cemetery just outside of town. The burial ground was located in a thickly wooded hollow which had been the setting for many scares in his youth, when he and his friends would roam through it seeking adventure. On this night, the man turned up his collar and walked very fast, frequently glancing over his shoulder.

As he neared the plot, he heard a rattling noise near a headstone. He peered curiously into the moonlit darkness in that direction. To his horror, he saw what appeared to be a white shape bobbing up and down close to the tombstone. He did not wait to investigate further, but hastily left for home and safety. When he arrived, he told his tale with much color and enthusiasm. Unfortunately he had told similar stories before, so the new thriller was met with less than wide-eyed attention. But he stuck to his tale.

A night or so later, another considerably more reliable resident of the area also saw the weird bobbing "ghost" by the headstone and heard the dry rattle in the moonlight. By now all the local residents began to pay attention to the frightening stories.

After a third sighting of the mysterious ghost in the burial plot, some of the braver males in town decided to set up a "ghost" watch near the grave, and they armed themselves for their vigil with a shotgun and a lantern with a protecting shield.

The first few nights passed quietly, and the "ghost watch" had nothing to report. But then, late one evening, they heard a muffled moan — a moan which resembled the soft lowing of a cow. Then they heard a dry rattle, and soon a white object began to bob up and down in the dark bushes by the gravestone.

The almost-but-not-quite petrified ghost hunters uncovered their lantern and prepared themselves to shoot if the need arose. They'd have done better with a milk pail, for the "ghost" turned out to be a white-faced black cow who had learned a new trick. She had discovered that if she stuck her head through the dry branches of a big old lilac bush by the headstone and bobbed her head up and down, she could scratch both sides of her neck at the same time.

The ghost hunters sneaked silently away, perhaps in search of a milking stool.

# Phantom Stagecoach

Many years ago there was a small Arizona frontier town that was kept alive by a gold mine nearby. The town had been on the stagecoach route, but when the mine petered out and was abandoned, the stage line was discontinued. The little town was almost completely cut off from the rest of the settlements. Only an infrequent freight line run by a local livery stable owner remained.

There was one young boy in the poverty-stricken town who was always exploring the nearby hills, hoping to find another mine to bring back the people who had moved away and also the stagecoach which he had loved. He had always been there to meet it when it came tearing into the little town in a cloud of dust.

The other people in town looked upon the boy's prospecting with amusement, but they did not bother him. In fact, they rather hoped that he would find a mine and really bring back prosperity.

One day the boy left for the hills as usual, with his burro and his lunch, but by nightfall he had not returned. As he had always been back by dark before, his folks became concerned. True, he was self-reliant and used to the rough living of the times and area, but anything might have happened. Finally, just after midnight, he came home, exhausted but excited. The stagecoach, he said, had come back to town after all.

Then he told this story. He had become separated from his burro back in the hills, and after searching for a long time he gave up and started home on foot. It was dark by the time he reached the old coach road to town, and he could hear the howls of wolves in the timber of the foothills close by. He hurried, but the cries of the wolves behind him became louder and louder. In panic he climbed to the top of a high rock by the roadside to wait for the pack to close in.

Just as the wolves approached, he heard the noise of a stagecoach coming along the old road. A dark stage drawn by black horses had pulled around the bend and come to a leather-creaking stop beside the rock where he sat in terror. The driver motioned for him to climb in, and then the coach raced toward town with the wolves howling right behind. It was quite a story for a young boy to make up, but the strangest part was to come to light the next day.

Just outside of town a huge gray wolf was found, obviously run over by a heavy wagon or stagecoach. The tracks of the vehicle came right to the edge of town, and then they stopped. They did not turn around and go back — they just stopped, as though they had vanished with the coach that made them. What had brought the boy back to safety was certainly something more substantial than mere imagination.

# The Haunted Bow

THIS TALE OF A MYSTERIOUS CURIO comes from the Isle of Man in the Irish Sea, between England and Ireland. Back about the turn of the century, Edward Kelly, a contractor, went from his home there to Australia to work. He was most successful, and in 1902 he returned to the Isle of Man to visit his brother in Port St. Mary.

As a gift to his brother he brought a fine native bow, some arrows, and a native spear which had been given to him by a sailor before he left Australia. The sailor was anxious to get rid of the bow, claiming that it had been cursed by its former owner, chief of one of the native tribes of the Trobriand Islands off the northern coast of British New Guinea, from whom it had been stolen by some British sailors.

At Mr. Kelly's brother's home, the bow was hung on a nail over the piano. But it refused to stay there. Almost at once strange whisperings, odd noises, and shadows flitting about the room kept the family in a constant state of nerves. One December evening, while Mr. Kelly's niece was playing the piano, the bow suddenly sprang from the wall and landed in the middle of the room behind the startled girl. It had not fallen from the nail — it had jumped several feet!

Mr. Kelly promptly hung it up and secured it with heavy copper wire, but a few days later it once more leaped from the wall, breaking the copper wire into shreds and making a great commotion as it did so. This time Mr. Kelly decided that he would be doubly certain that it stayed upon the wall. He added two more heavy nails and secured it by the ends as well as at the middle with extra-strong braided copper wire. No curse from far-off Australia would affect it again. Yet the weird noises and whisperings continued. A few nights later a terrific crash occurred, waking the entire family. Upon investigation they found all three wire strands broken and the bow in the middle of the room. This time Mr. Kelly decided not to bother with wires. He hung the bow back on the nails without bindings.

From that day on nothing more happened, and everyone wondered what had brought about this sudden calm. Mr. Kelly was convinced that on the date of the violent leap from the wall, the old chief who had owned the bow must either have died or had great need for it. He watched the papers and bulletins and finally found a clue. During an uprising, he read, the old chief had been captured, deprived of his weapons, and thrown into jail by the Australian police. This happened in December, 1902, the very month of the strange happenings so far away on the Isle of Man.

Whether the chief died in jail or was executed was never determined, but apparently his need for weapons (if you like to believe in a bit of witchcraft) caused the faithful bow to try to go to his assistance. Or perhaps his spirit came across the trackless seas to try to bring it back.

# Warning of Disaster

THERE IS A PIECE OF BROKEN TILE on my bookcase shelf — not a particularly pretty tile, with about one-third missing. It is made of light tan pottery with a thin white glaze over it. Burned into this white glaze is a quaint, light blue picture of a trumpeter on horseback outside the gates of a walled city. Another horseman and assorted figures are in the background. It's not a very exciting picture, and certainly not a valuable tile. But it is a souvenir of one of the greatest disasters of all time, in which it is reported that 40,000 people died, 28,000 of them instantly.

This tile came from the ruins of St. Pierre on the island of Martinique. St. Pierre was completely destroyed by the explosion of Mt. Pelee in May, 1902. This active volcano, 4,500 feet high, had erupted several times before, but with lesser damage. This time it blew apart completely! The only survivor of the great disaster was a lone prisoner in an underground dungeon. That anyone should survive was so miraculous that this man was brought to America and exhibited by P. T. Barnum. But this story is not about him.

All that remains today of the great catastrophe is a museum of relics — and an unusual tale of warning before the disaster occurred.

J. W. Dunne was a British military engineer who was greatly interested in dreams and their meanings. He kept careful records of all of his unusual dreams to see if they might possibly foretell future events. In the spring of 1902 he was stationed with the Mounted Infantry in the Orange Free State, South Africa.

One night he had a particularly disturbing dream, which upset him greatly. He dreamed that he had been stationed upon an island that only he knew was about to explode. He tried frantically to induce the French authorities to evacuate the people in time, but they laughed at his suggestion and ignored his pleas. He tried again and again to warn the people of their danger, but they too laughed at him. And the island did explode, killing everyone. In his dream, nearly 40,000 were killed, as he had warned.

He awoke in a cold sweat, trembling with panic. He hurriedly wrote down all the details of his dream — just in case.

A few days later, newspapers were delivered to his outpost in Africa. All of them headlined the great explosion which had devastated St. Pierre, killing 40,000 people just as he had dreamed.

To answer the old question, "What's in a dream?" — sometimes something mysterious and terrible, and *true!*

# The Vanishing Riverboat

THERE IS SOMETHING FRIGHTENINGLY MYSTERIOUS about the sudden disappearance of people or things. This is particularly true when there is no way to explain it. One moment they are there, and the next they have vanished without trace. One such vanishing act has remained an unsolved mystery for almost a century.

It happened in June of 1872 near Vicksburg, Mississippi, on the great winding Mississippi River. This was the era when stern-wheelers were thick upon the muddy waters. The *Iron Mountain* was one of these — a monster of a boat, with a length of nearly 180 feet and a beam (width) of 35 feet. She was powered with five huge boilers, and was only eight years old at the time.

This day in June, she stopped off at Vicksburg on her way from New Orleans to Pittsburgh, loaded with cotton and molasses. She was towing a string of loaded barges, as was the custom of many riverboats.

She completed her business at Vicksburg, unloaded her passengers, and took on more for the trip upriver.

Then she pulled away from the dock. Her barges swung out behind her as her great twin stacks belched smoke and sparks, and she headed north around the bend in the river — into oblivion.

What happened around that bend will never be known, for the *Iron Mountain* completely vanished — passengers, crew, cargo, and all. All that remained was a string of barges.

The first sign of anything unusual was when another steamer, the *Iroquois Chief*, had to swing out of the way of a string of drifting barges coming downstream from around that bend in the great river. She turned and caught the barges and finally brought them to a halt. She expected another steamer to come and claim them, but none did. Later examination showed that the tow cable had been cut, not broken — an action usually taken in an emergency to save a steamer at the expense of losing the barges. These were the barges that had been behind the *Iron Mountain*. But what had happened to her?

There was not the slightest sign of debris, either from the huge ship itself, its deck-piled cargo, or its many passengers and crew. There was no sound or smoke from a vast explosion or fire, no floating bodies or wreckage. If she had suddenly sunk, some debris, bodies, or cargo would surely have come to the surface.

The great ship, her cargo, and the 55 persons aboard had utterly vanished from the face of the earth. To this day no one knows how, why, or where they went.

# Great Lakes Gold

LOST OR BURIED TREASURE almost automatically brings forth a picture of palm trees, white sands, and tropical waters. But exotic islands are not the only sites of long-lost treasure. In the Great Lakes area alone, hundreds of ships have gone down with valuable cargoes. Along the shores of the inland lakes, too, treasure and gold have been buried for one reason or another and never found again.

Just to the east of a point of land running out into the western tip of Lake Superior are the Apostle Islands. On the mainland is the city of Bayfield, Wisconsin, and a short distance out into the lake is one of the smaller of these islands, Hermit Island.

In the early days of the United States much fighting between the British and American troops took place around this area. There were also small but bitter skirmishes between the British and hostile Indians.

A small British outpost on Hermit Island was the target of a good-sized Indian force. The soldiers were particularly concerned, for they were guarding the payroll for many of the British troops in that part of the country. Exactly how much gold and silver made up this payroll is not known, but it is rumored to have been considerable.

As the Indian attack seemed more and more imminent, the officers decided to bury the money for safekeeping. A small group of trusted officers took the treasure to a remote part of the little island and buried it well. After covering up all signs of the digging, they returned to the main force to await the attack.

A bloody battle ensued, and all but two of the British soldiers were massacred on the spot. The two enlisted men who survived were badly wounded, but they managed to reach the mainland with news of the slaughter. The men knew about the burial of the payroll, but they had no idea where on the island it was hidden.

To this day the treasure has not been found. Somewhere on this little island in Lake Superior a hoard of old coins may still rest below the soil, guarded by roots and rocks that have shifted over it during the years. It may even be further guarded by the ghosts of those who thought they were hiding it for a few days instead of forever.

# Ice from Heaven

LATE ONE WARM JULY AFTERNOON, a Pennsylvania farmer was working outdoors when he suddenly heard a loud whistling sound from overhead. Then something huge crashed into the ground a short distance away and smashed into a shower of broken pieces. When he could collect his wits, he hastened to the spot and found that an area about 60 feet in diameter was covered with what looked like shattered ice.

Upon examination, he found that it really was ice — but of a peculiar, milky-white, china-like color. He rushed back to the house to tell his wife, and they both returned to the field. As they stood looking at the broken chunks of ice, another whistle was heard, and then, about 50 yards away, another smaller piece of ice crashed to the ground. No aircraft had flown over, there had been no thunderstorms, and there was nothing unusual about the sky.

The farmer and his wife collected the pieces of ice and hurriedly brought them to the house, where they were stored in the deep-freeze. They had a chemist study the fragments and check for radioactivity. The results were never disclosed, and it could only be guessed that what had fallen to the ground on that warm summer day were two of the largest hailstones ever seen by any man.

# Babe in the Woods

FREQUENTLY WE READ of youngsters wandering away from picnic parties and becoming lost in the woods. This is stark tragedy for the parents, even in this day of helicopters, bloodhounds, and state police.

In pioneer days a youngster lost in the woods was due for almost certain death. Prowling Indians and wild animals were common, and there were no organized rescue facilities. It was almost a miracle when a lost child was found alive. Almost a miracle?

In June, 1783, a couple living in Warren, New Hampshire, set out to walk the mile or so to a neighbor's house near the summit of a low mountain to the north. Their four-year-old daughter Sarah begged to be taken along, but they decided to leave her home with the older children. As they started off along the trail following Berry Brook, neither realized that Sarah had slipped away after them. The little girl soon lost the trail and wandered into the woods. After a while, tired and scratched by briers, she curled up by a big rock and fell asleep.

Just as night was falling, the parents returned home. To their horror they discovered that Sarah was gone. The other children, sure she was with her parents, had not been alarmed. It was beginning to rain as the frantic father called his neighbors to aid in the search.

73

They combed the woods until dawn, but found no trace of the small child.

From Sunday until Wednesday the search went on. Dozens of men looked night and day for some sign of the child. On Thursday a strange thing occurred — almost a supernatural event.

About noon on that day a man named Heath, from Plymouth, 20 miles away, strode up to the cabin and said, "Give me some dinner and I will find the child." As he ate he told about a vivid dream he had had three times the night before. In his dream, he had found the lost child under a big pine tree southwest of Berry Brook, guarded by a huge bear.

The neighbors looked at each other in astonishment, for it was true that some of the men had found the child's tracks along with those of a large bear, but they had not mentioned this to the distraught parents. The implication had been too horrible.

Mr. Heath and another settler went off into the woods, heading straight for the spot in the dream. Hours later the waiting group heard three gunshots. This was to be the signal if the child was found.

The two men had indeed found Sarah asleep under a pine tree. But the dream prediction was incomplete, for there had been no sign of a bear guarding her.

Later, when Sarah was warm and rested, she was asked about her adventure. Then she told how she had awakened from her nap the day she lost her way to find a "big black dog" sniffing at her scratched legs. She told of how she had put her arms about its neck and how each night the "big black dog" had come back and had lain down beside her to keep her warm.

# Lost Countries

TALES OF LOST CONTINENTS, vanished cities, and sunken countries have contributed to folklore and legend throughout history. Many of these tales, of course, are pure legend, but there are others which may very well be true. We know that the floor of the ocean rises and settles sometimes in great upheavals, causing huge tidal waves. Great alterations in topography often follow.

In 1924 a cable-repair ship was sent to fix a break in a line between Cape Town and St. Helena. The location of the break was determined to be about 800 miles north of Cape Town, where the cable entered the water.

When this section of the cable had been laid in 1899 it was a bit over three miles below the surface. Consequently the cable-repair ship began to pay out line and grapnels — hooks to grasp the cables — at that depth. But they struck bottom and picked up the cable at a depth of only three-quarters of a mile. Within 25 years that part of the ocean floor had risen more than two miles. If, instead, it had sunk as much, the coastline might well have been altered, and cities may have vanished beneath the ocean. This is what apparently happened to the long string of "lost" islands known on old charts as Davisland, off the west coast of South America.

In 1688 a Dutch seafaring man named Wafer reported on a voyage he had taken the year before, as first mate of the British ship *The Bachelor's Delight* under the command of Captain John Davis.

During that voyage, at approximately 27 degrees, 20 minutes south, Wafer sighted an unknown chain of islands to the northwest. This chain seemed to extend to the north about 15 leagues (about 40 miles).

Captain Davis corroborated Wafer's report and the land was named Davisland in his honor. The crew did not explore the islands because they were anxious to get home, but Davisland was put on all navigation charts of the area. The islands have never been seen since!

Some experts have thought that this vanished archipelago may have been the home of the people who carved the mysterious statues on Easter Island. Someday we may know the answer to the mystery, but in the meantime we know that there are vanished lands beneath the seas. Perhaps they will rise again.

# The Story of John Wilson

John Wilson was a rather shiftless individual who made a meager living by doing odd jobs, hunting, and fishing. The year was 1840, the place was an island in Casco Bay, Maine.

Deciding one day to do some duck hunting on neighboring Elm Island, John loaded his shotgun, powder horn and shot, and a small lunch into his leaky old boat, and rowed across. It was to be an eventful day.

He dragged his boat up onto the rocky shore, above the high-tide mark, and set out for a place where he knew ducks could usually be found. This day he had a long wait for his first duck, but finally he managed to bag one and hastily stuffed it in a safe place while he reloaded his gun to be ready for the next target.

While he waited, he opened his scanty lunch and began eating slowly to make it last longer, keeping an eye on the water. Little did he know just how close he crouched to adventure and excitement.

Presently a lone duck came gliding toward the little cove before him. He quickly put down his food and raised his ancient weapon. On came the bird. He took aim and fired. Then, peering though the cloud of stinging smoke from the old muzzle-loader, he spotted his bird. Wounded but alive, it was flopping about among the slippery rocks above the beach. Heedless of his safety, Wilson scrambled after his quarry, his powder horn on its rawhide thong bouncing and bobbing against his ragged old coat.

Suddenly, as he raced across a ledge, his feet plunged into a kelp-filled hole and he went down sprawling, his hat flying off and his old gun clattering on the ledge. For a moment he lay there, stunned. When he realized that his quarry was escaping, he clawed frantically at the wet, slippery kelp that filled the hole almost to his waist. His hand closed about a stiff stalk, and he pulled hard to free himself.

It was not a kelp stalk he had grasped. It was the handle of an old copper kettle hidden in the crevice of the ledge — a kettle full of old coins — twelve thousand dollars worth. How they got there will never be known, but John Wilson, according to the story, spent the rest of his life in ease — something he had mastered long ago.

# The Devil Comes to Church

THE CONGREGATION CHURCH in Ipswich, Massachusetts, is the fifth to stand on its present site. The first, built in 1640, was the scene of an interesting and fantastic legend about a fight between a minister, the Reverend George Whitefield of England, and the devil himself. It is all faithfully recorded in the history of the town, and some of the evidence is still there to see.

It was in 1740 that Reverend Whitefield went on a tour of New England villages. In each town he preached a resounding sermon, calling on the citizens to put down the devil and all his teachings. When he arrived in Ipswich, a great crowd awaited him and the church overflowed.

According to the records, his sermon was so powerful that the devil himself decided he'd better get up here and hear what the minister had to say. In the middle of the sermon he arrived, complete with horns and a long tail. It took him only a moment to decide that he had better stop the sermon before he lost face altogether. And so he challenged Reverend Whitefield to a wrestling match to decide who was the better man.

They fought all over the floor of the church, rolled outside, and finally worked their way up the steep sides of the steeple. Before the horrified throngs below they strove to push each other off the peak of the spire to certain destruction on the ledges below. It looked pretty bad for the Reverend Whitefield, until with a mighty heave he shoved the devil from the steeple. Down he fell, straight for the rocky ledge jutting out of the grassy hill (A in the sketch).

Just as he seemed about to crash into the ledge, head first, Satan righted himself and landed with a thundering crash upon his feet. As he hit the ledge of granite, he sent up a shower of smoke and sparks. Then, with a great cry, he leaped off down the hill and was never seen in Ipswich again.

Even today the devil's footprint remains in the rock ledge (B). During my visit there, in a moment of bravado I slipped off my shoe to try it for size. My stockinged foot fitted the deep imprint of the devil's footprint — perfectly.

# The Sawdust Pile

A TRAIN I WAS ON not too long ago had just rumbled past a huge sawdust pile almost hidden in the New England woods. You've probably seen such sawdust piles, with the ruins of an old sawmill close by.

Well, as we passed this long-forgotten pile, I heard the man next to me mutter, "I wonder where it went." A moment later he turned to me and asked if I believed in the supernatural. My interest aroused, I asked him what he meant. This is what he told me:

When he was a boy he had lived in a western state where there had been much lumbering. Near his home in the country a huge sawdust pile, some broken buildings and sheds, and a sagging tin smokestack were all that remained of a vast lumbering operation that had once taken place there. One winter snow fell heavily, and the youngsters decided to slide down the snow-covered sawdust pile on their sleds into the field below. They had great fun until the snow wore thin and the sawdust stopped their sleds.

A few days later more snow arrived, and after school the same children grabbed their sleds and headed through the woods and across the fields for some more rides from the top of the huge pile. They whooped and yelled as they ploughed knee-deep through the snow toward the field. But when they reached the spot, their shouts suddenly faded into silence.

There was no snow-covered sawdust pile there, but only the ruins of the old mill and a vacant clearing. The giant mound of sawdust, which had covered nearly an acre and towered to perhaps 30 feet, had vanished. They knew they were in the right place, for there was the wreck of the old mill and the chimney, but where were the tons of sawdust? There were no tracks in the snow, nor had the parents of the bewildered youngsters heard of anyone's removing the pile. Surely, if this had been done, someone in the area would have known about it.

My travelling companion fell silent. I asked him, then, if he had ever returned to look for traces of the sawdust. Yes, he replied, he had gone back in the summertime, to find the ground covered with pretty yellow-orange flowers strange to that region. "What kind of flowers were they?" I asked. He smiled a bit, with an amused and faraway look. "I believe they are called Devil's Paintbrushes," he said.

# The Witch on the Colt's Neck

THIS STORY WAS TOLD by an old doctor who used to live a hermit's life in a small New England village. It happened when he was a young boy, but he told it and retold it in exactly the same way until his death. To him it was frighteningly true.

When the doctor was a young man of fifteen, his father had a bay colt which he permitted the youngster to ride. One evening the boy left his home and started riding to another town a few miles away. On the way he had to pass a cottage where a woman by the name of Dolly Spokesfield lived. She was rumored to have unusual powers, skill in the black arts and the ability to turn herself into almost anything she wished. She was, it was whispered, a genuine witch of the inner circle — certainly a person to be avoided by young boys out at night alone.

As the lad approached Dolly Spokesfield's cottage he kept to the middle of the road and nervously urged the colt to a faster trot. But his precautions were in vain.

As the colt and rider came abreast of the cottage, a coal black cat suddenly leaped out of the darkness and landed on the colt's neck. The frightened horse stopped short, almost throwing the boy over his head. The boy tried desperately to get rid of the cat and urged his mount on, beating him with his whip, but the cat held on and the colt refused to move with the black cat hissing upon his neck.

The boy was afraid to leave his horse and run, and in panic he dismounted and began to beat the cat with the whip, holding the colt by the bridle rein as he reared and plunged, trying to shake off the cat.

At last the boy managed to dislodge the cat and he hurriedly rode home. The poor colt was bruised and clawed by the cat, and apparently exhausted by his ordeal. So injured and frightened was he that the boy was afraid the animal would die before morning. He turned him loose in the barn instead of putting him in the stall, and went to bed trembling and fearful that the colt wouldn't last the night.

At the first crack of dawn, the boy arose and hurried to the barn to inspect the battered and clawed animal. To his amazement, the young horse was in perfect condition. He showed no signs of exhaustion, and nowhere on his body could the boy find a trace of bruises from the whip, a claw mark, or a single reminder of the frantic events of the previous night.

However, the story had an even stranger ending. A neighbor soon stopped by to report that Dolly Spokesfield had just been found almost dead, her body bruised and beaten as though by a whip. And under two of her fingernails were some short bay hairs, such as you'd find, perhaps, on the neck of a young colt ridden by a frightened boy alone in the night.

# Lord Dufferin's Story

LORD DUFFERIN, a British diplomat, was the central figure of this story, which has become one of England's classic tales of the supernatural.

One night during a stay at a friend's country house in Ireland, Lord Dufferin was unusually restless and could not sleep. He had an inexplicable feeling of dread, and so, to calm his nerves, he arose and walked across the room to the window.

A full moon illuminated the garden below so that it was almost as bright as morning, as Lord Dufferin stood there by the window. Suddenly he was conscious of a movement in the shadows and a man appeared, carrying a long box on his back. The silent and sinister figure walked slowly across the moonlit yard. As he

85

passed the window from which Lord Dufferin intently watched, he stopped and looked directly into the diplomat's eyes.

Lord Dufferin recoiled, for the face of the man carrying the burden was so ugly that he could not even describe it later. For a moment their eyes met, and then the man moved off into the shadows. The box on his back was clearly seen to be a casket.

The next morning Dufferin asked his host and the other guests about the man in the garden, but no one knew anything about him. He was even accused of having a nightmare, but he knew better.

Many years later in Paris, when Lord Dufferin was serving as the English ambassador to France, he was about to step into an elevator on the way to an important meeting of diplomats. For some unexpected reason he glanced at the elevator operator, and with a violent start recognized the man he had seen carrying the coffin across the moonlit garden. Involuntarily he stepped back from the elevator and stood there as the door closed and it started up without him.

His agitation was so great that he remained motionless for several minutes. Then a terrific crash startled him. The cable had parted, and the elevator had fallen three floors to the basement. Several passengers were killed in the tragedy and the operator himself died.

Investigation revealed that the operator had been hired for just that day, and no one has ever known who he was or where he came from.

# The Old Chief's Tomahawk

IN AMERICA'S OLD WEST, tomahawks were often the instrument of death for many courageous pioneers. Once, however, this weapon played an exciting and mysterious part in saving a child from a tragic end.

A hardy settler and his equally plucky family lived in a cabin far out in the wilderness. Wolves frequently raided the flocks and were even known to attack people when hunger made them ravenous. To add to the dangers, Indians still roamed the area, looking for whatever they could steal. Occasionally they attacked a cabin, burned it and killed the inhabitants. It took great courage to live in such a place.

One day the seven-year-old daughter of the family came upon a very old and sick Indian in the woods. Instead of running away in panic, she helped the ancient man to the cabin and pleaded with her folks to care for him. In spite of misgivings, her parents agreed, but it soon became evident that he did not have long to live.

87

Although the old chief could speak no English, he and the little girl became fast friends. She did everything she could to make his last days comfortable and he was obviously very grateful. Just before he died he called the girl and her parents to his bedside. Giving his tomahawk to the child, he motioned to the father to hang it on the wall over her small bunk. His wish was granted, although the family could not understand why he wanted this done.

Some weeks later, while the father and mother were both away and the little girl was napping in her bunk, a gaunt wolf slipped out of the forest and headed for the cabin. He slunk up to the door, sniffed a few times, and then pushed against it. It swung open and he started to enter, his yellow eyes intent upon the tiny girl asleep in the bunk before him.

When the parents returned, they were horrified to see a huge wolf apparently crawling into their cabin. They raced across the clearing, shouting, but the wolf did not move. For he was dead, his skull crushed from a terrible blow upon the head. Their daughter was still asleep in her bunk.

Later, the father jokingly said that perhaps the old chief had come back to protect the little girl with his tomahawk. Something impelled him to lift the crude weapon from its peg over the bunk. As he looked at it, his laughter ceased.

The blade was splotched with dried blood and in the rawhide thong binding the primitive blade to the stout handle were several long gray hairs, such as might be found on the head of a timber wolf!

# The Indian Guide

IN THE PIONEER DAYS OF THE OLD WEST a family had settled on the edge of a wide forest. Close by in the woods lived an old Indian couple who were very friendly. The old Indians and the little daughter of the pioneer family were particularly fond of one another.

One winter, when the youngster was about six, she started off to visit another little girl who lived in a cabin about a mile away through the woods. She had gone there alone many times before, so her parents thought nothing of her making the trip again, even though it was winter and it looked as if it would snow. There were few wild animals in the forest, and no wolves had been in the area for many years.

Bundled up in leggings and shawl over her head, the child started off. Her parents were not concerned until they realized that it was growing dark and she was not back. When her father stepped out into the twilight to see if he could see her or hear her coming, he found, to his dismay, that it was snowing quite heavily. There was no sign of his small daughter.

At once he and his oldest boy hurried into their heaviest wraps, took a lantern and their musket, and started off at a trot down the trail to the other cabin. As they ran along they kept calling the little girl's name, but their only reply was the howling of the wind and an occasional hoot from a great gray owl.

At the neighbor's house they learned that the little girl had left some time ago, before the snow began, and should have arrived home long ago. Their alarm mounted. But perhaps, they reasoned, she had left the trail to visit the hut of the old Indian couple.

The girl's brother set forth to visit the Indians, and her father and the neighbors headed homeward, fanning out through the dark woods to see if they might find the girl before the snow and storm covered up all tracks.

The men reached home first and were overjoyed to find the little girl safe by the fire, drinking some hot broth while her mother dried her clothes. She had lost her way, she told them, and after stumbling in the drifts for a while she had started to cry. Almost at once her old Indian friend had appeared and led her home, holding her tiny hand in his all the way, until they could see the lights of her cabin ahead. Then he had smiled at her and vanished into the dark woods behind them.

Then her brother returned from the Indians' hut with a sad tale. There, he said, he had found the old squaw huddled by the body of her brave, who had died two days before.

# The Bewitched Cat of the Catskills

IN THE EARLY DAYS OF OUR COUNTRY, many tales of witchcraft originated in the Catskill Mountain area of New York. Take the one about the cats of Spook Woods.

Spook Woods deserved its name, for everyone knew that it was full of mystery. In fact, it was said that even dull-witted cattle who wandered into the woods would suddenly rush away in panic at what they had encountered. Certainly horses often balked at taking the road which ran through Spook Woods. The local people usually managed to go through Spook Woods only in broad daylight, and preferably with company.

A farmhand named Williams, the story goes, had been hired to work on a farm on the other side of the woods from his home. Williams had heard tales of Spook Woods, as who up that way hadn't. But he was a big, rugged, and ordinarily fearless man who paid little attention to the tales of witches, spooks, and supernatural happenings in the deep shadows.

However, one winter night as he returned home through the woods on foot, he did feel a certain uneasiness. Perhaps it was because of the full moon which cast odd shadows along the side of the dirt road, he reassured himself. But as he reached the center of the wooded stretch, he realized that one shadow was hurrying along ahead of him. This shadow was more than a trick of moonlight, for it was moving quickly over the snow along the roadside.

As he hurried to pass it, he saw to his astonishment that the shadow was made by two cats who were dragging an obviously dead cat between them. What a strange way for animals to act, he thought, as he quickened his steps to pass them. The cats hurried too and kept right up with him. Then, to his increasing horror, one of them called him by name. Startled as he was, he wouldn't — he couldn't — stop. The terrified man began to run, desperately anxious to get out of the woods as fast as possible.

The cats, slowed down by their burden, could not match his speed, but just as he was leaving the thick woods for the open country beyond, one of them screeched in a loud, clear, and almost human voice, "Mr. Williams, oh, Mr. Williams, when you get home tell Molly Meyers that she can come home now. Old man Hawkins is dead."

Terribly shaken by his experience, Mr. Williams raced on to the security of his home, but when he reached its warm, friendly atmosphere, he hesitated to tell his harrowing experience. Later in the evening, when his family was sitting around the fireplace, he half jokingly told about it, and finally repeated the odd message one of the cats had cried out after him.

To everyone's astonishment, the old white cat lying by the hearth sprang to her feet, and without once looking back, leaped up the chimney right over the burning logs and was never seen again. Had Molly Meyers at last gone home?

# The Balls of Clay

WHILE ON VACATION IN FLORIDA, a young man spent
a lot of time wandering along the sparsely populated
parts of the coastline looking for interesting odds and
ends — unusual shells, pieces of driftwood, and bits
of wreckage from ships.

On one of these beachcombing trips he happened
to notice a small hole partway up a low cliff. Curious,
he climbed up and looked into the opening. Perhaps
a pirate treasure or hidden chest might be there.

He peered into the long tapering passage which
ran a couple of feet back into the ledge, but he could
see nothing in the gloom of the tiny "cave." Cautiously
he put his hand into the far corners to see if anything
had been tucked far back. Sure enough, against the
back wall of the opening, his hand touched what felt
like bird's eggs or marbles — a little pile of them.

Picking up a handful, he brought them into the light

to look at. They varied from about the size of a large pea to almost the size of a golf ball, and they were round and smooth and apparently made of a hard gray clay-like substance. Certainly they had no value, he thought in disappointment, but he filled his pockets with about two dozen "marbles" and climbed down to the sandy shore below.

As he walked along the beach he occasionally threw one of the clay balls at floating driftwood or stopped a moment to see how many "skips" a ball made as he skittered it out over the surface of the ocean. Finally they were all gone.

A few days later the visitor returned to his home in the Midwest. As he was unpacking his vacation clothes, he discovered one of the clay balls, overlooked in the bottom of his pocket, and tossed it into a drawer as a souvenir of his "find" in the cliff cave.

Not long after, he and a friend who was interested in pirate lore were talking about some of the famous buccaneers who had hidden treasure along the Florida coasts. When his friend told him that some of the pirates used to hide precious stones in small clay balls, he described how he had found such balls in the little cave. They laughed over what he had done with the "precious stones" — and forgot the incident.

Afterward, when he remembered the small pellet he had saved, his curiosity was aroused. Quickly he took his souvenir and began to scrape away the hardened clay. At first there was nothing but clay. Then the mass cracked — and out rolled a small but perfect blue-white diamond. What had been in the other clay balls which he had thrown far into the sea?

# Moonlight Ghost of Middleton

THE MOONLIGHT GHOST OF MIDDLETON had a whole village in England mystified for many years. It was in Durham County that a very odd ghost appeared in the corner of a certain field whenever the moon was full. Many people had seen the dancing, flickering, ghostly light, but no one had dared to cross the moonlit field to challenge the apparition. Daylight revealed nothing unusual in the field. But every month when the moon was full — and only then — the ghost could be seen from certain points. It wasn't long before the village folks avoided those places from where the specter was visible, for rumor held that it was bad luck to even see the moonlight ghost. It was even wiser, the people thought, to whisper about the moonlight ghost than to talk about it in public in loud and disbelieving tones.

But there was one man who refused to whisper. This rugged individualist, Robert Bainbridge by name, had intelligence as well as brawn. He feared hardly a man alive and would not tremble before a flickering spirit who hadn't enough gumption to show himself in broad daylight. Scoffing contemptuously at the tales of the moonlight ghost, and ignoring the warnings and sneers of the villagers, he decided to settle the matter for once and all.

On a night when the moon was full, he approached the field. There, in the corner, he too saw the flickering apparition. Now was his chance. With a quickening pulse, Robert Bainbridge strode to the corner where the dancing phantom flickered and wavered. It did not flee before him, nor did it vanish. It stayed there as if waiting for him.

Robert Bainbridge must have burst into a relieved laugh at what he saw. For the ghost was the reflection of the moon dancing on the surface of a long-forgotten well hidden in the grass. And so the mystery of Middleton's moonlight ghost was solved. The villagers, however, were not relieved. In fact, they resented the solution, for they had grown rather fond of the haunted field and the flickering neighbor who had lived there so long.

# The Army That Disappeared

IN 1939, CHINA AND JAPAN were at war. On December 10, Japanese soldiers were marching on the Chinese city of Nanking, and the Chinese desperately attempted to hold them off as long as possible. To the south of Nanking rolling hills offered a chance for a last-ditch stand against the advancing Japanese, if extra troops could be obtained to take up defensive positions there.

Answering the request for aid, 3,100 Chinese troops

were rushed to the hills. Sixteen miles from an important junction near the only bridge across the river, they dug in for a fight to the finish. During the night the troops, with six or seven howitzers, spread out along a line two miles long. They were well hidden against any aerial attack that might come. The commander, Colonel Li Fu Sien, personally inspected the men and then retired to his own headquarters a mile behind the lines.

An hour or so later, just before dawn, the colonel was awakened by an aide, who told him that he had been unable to contact the right flank of the new defense line. There was no reply to any signals, and the aide suggested that the colonel make another trip to see what was the matter.

To his amazement, the colonel found nothing. With the exception of one small group stationed at an outpost near the bridge, every man had vanished.

The men at the outpost had heard no sounds during the night, and there were no signs of a struggle anywhere along the line. The guns were still in place, and many of the small campfires were still burning. No one had crossed the only bridge that led to the Japanese lines, and the area had been so blasted by shell fire that the only trees left offered no shelter if the men had sneaked off in cowardice.

Even if, somehow, they had been able to reach the enemy lines in a mass surrender, there would have been some record of it in Japanese reports. There was no such mention, and what is even more mysterious, not one of the 2,988 Chinese soldiers was ever seen or heard of again.

# Amelia Island Legend

THE CITY OF FERNANDINA, on Amelia Island, Florida, is noted for its past history of pirate legend and buried treasure. Such famous figures as Captain Kidd and Edward Teach ("Blackbeard") were among those reputed to have used Amelia Island as a place of safekeeping for their ill-gotten gains. Two onlookers actually *saw* treasure being buried, yet were powerless to do anything about it.

The two witnesses were Negro slaves. In 1788 they were taken captive and put on a slave ship, but they jumped overboard, swam ashore, and took refuge on the island. Some time later they saw a ship approaching. Thinking it might be another slave ship coming to look for them, they hid where they could watch the shore but could not be seen. The ship anchored offshore, a small boat was put over, and a group of sailors rowed toward the island where the men lay hidden.

Concealed in the thick underbrush, they watched the sailors unload two large chests from the boat and stagger off into the undergrowth with them. It took eight men to carry the two chests, which were obviously very heavy. The escaped slaves watched the pirates carry the heavy chests about 300 yards inland where there was a deer trail leading through the brush to a small pond to the west. Here the men lowered the chests to the ground and set about preparing a resting place for it.

While the hidden men watched, the diggers worked in relays. When the hole was completed they once more hoisted the chests off the ground, and with many a grunt and much loud swearing, some of which was in a foreign tongue, they lowered the two chests to the bottom of the pit.

Then they shoveled the dirt over the hole, packed down the surface firmly, and carefully smoothed it so it looked as if it had never been disturbed. Grass and leaves and light brush were cleverly dropped and scattered over the hidden chests, so that in a few moments the spot on the deer trail was as natural as ever. Soon the pirates rowed back to their ship and sailed past the horizon.

Only the pirates and the two men who watched from the underbrush knew about the buried treasure. The men never returned to the site, for fear of finding the pirates there or of being caught with the treasure and being accused of robbery or worse. Since no one ever reported finding it, it may still be there on Amelia Island.

# Marie Antoinette's Necklace

AMONG THE MANY TALES of vanished treasure that fill the pages of history, there is the legend of Marie Antoinette's fabulous diamond necklace.

Just before the French Revolution, two jewelers in league with two cardinals forced Marie Antoinette to purchase the magnificent necklace. Its price was six million pounds.

During the hectic days of the Revolution, the cardinals feared for the necklace's safety and had it sent secretly to England. From there it was sent to Canada, the haven of many exiled Frenchmen. Its fate after that was never explained, and history does not record its final resting place — or perhaps it does.

Toward the end of the 18th century a Frenchman, accompanied by an Indian, came from Canada to a small town near what is now Nashua, New Hampshire. The two lived in a little hut on a wood road leading to Pennichuck Pond. All the years he lived there, the Frenchman gave the impression that he had some great secret, but no one knew what it was. From time to time the Indian went back to Canada, and then months later he returned. During his absence the Frenchman left his hut only for food or other vital supplies. Occasionally he walked along the edge of the little pond, apparently deep in thought.

While the Indian was away on one of his periodical trips, the Frenchman died. When the Indian returned, he was greatly upset over the death of his companion, and left again after a few days.

Some years later, he came back again. Carefully, trying not to arouse suspicion, he began to make guarded inquiries about a beautiful string of wampum. It had been in the care of the Frenchman, he said, in trust for officials in Canada. When the two first arrived, they had buried it somewhere along the shore of Pennichuck Pond. Now he couldn't find it.

No one knew anything about the string of wampum. But the local people had heard of the famous diamond necklace, bought years ago in a far-off land. Had that been what the Frenchman was guarding?

A long and excited search began, but to this day no one knows if somewhere along the shores of tiny Pennichuck Pond a "string of wampum," the fabulous necklace of Marie Antoinette, still lies buried beneath the soil.

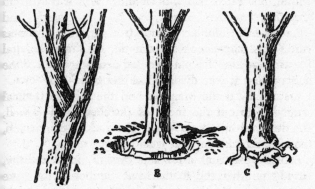

# The Suicide Tree

WOULD YOU LIKE TO SEE A TREE that is committing suicide?" This was asked by a friend who knew of my interest in the unusual and perhaps macabre.

Sure enough, when I arrived I was shown a tree that was bent on destroying itself. As I have sketched at *A*, a mulberry tree was killing itself by splitting the main trunk as another section was forced through the center. This section had grown from its point of origin, apparently seeking sunlight, and pushed back through the crotch of the other two sections. Over the years, as it grew larger and larger, it became deeply embedded and kept widening the split. The sap of the tree is running out through the split; and water, ice, and insects are entering to damage the tree from

103

within. Soon it will die, a victim of its own twisted growth.

I once had a similar "suicide tree" in my own front yard. This maple took its own life by strangulation. I wasn't aware of what had happened when I first noticed that it was dying. Deciding to take it down, I first removed the branches and then dug a trench around it to cut the roots, as sketched at B. But I couldn't find any roots at all. If I rocked the tree, I thought, the hidden roots would be revealed, so I tied a cable to the trunk a few feet over my head and secured the other end to the front bumper of my car.

With an eye on the tree trunk and the ground about its base, I slowly backed down the drive, expecting to see the ground hump up over the roots below. That was when I got my big surprise!

As soon as the cable received a strong tug, the tree started to come right toward the car. As if eager to crush me, it kept coming perilously closer. I backed down the drive faster and faster, and got to the end just as the tree fell, missing my front bumper by inches.

When my heart slowed down, I examined the bottom of the tree trunk and found something very strange. There hadn't been any roots to cut. As sketched at C, one large root (X) had completely encircled the base of the trunk, killing all but a few tiny roots. Then this root too had died, leaving nothing to feed the tree or hold it upright.

Why it stood as long as it did will always amaze me, for it was nothing but a trunk standing in a couple of feet of earth. One good windstorm would have toppled it.

# The Lost City of Machu Picchu

IN THE YEAR 1535, when Pizarro and his Spanish soldiers warred on the Incas of Peru, the Indians were driven back further and further and built a fabulous city in a most secret place high in the mountains. This city is now called Machu Picchu, after the mountain upon which it was secretly constructed. It was a fantastic place, built of granite blocks, cleverly fitted together to last forever as a stronghold of the vanishing race.

To this city retired the last of the Inca leaders, warriors and maidens, after the plundering and murdering of Pizarro's men had driven them into the hills. The vast hidden city was never visited by a

105

stranger, and only the Incas knew of its location 8,000 feet up in the peaks of the Andes Mountains.

Finally the last of the warriors, descending into the valley for food, were ambushed in the canyons at the base of the mountain. Only the old people and maidens remained in the hidden city. It wasn't long before silence fell over the great granite city with its buildings and plazas, for none dared to go to the valley for food or help.

That silence continued for more than three centuries. The few who knew the location of the city refused to tell. Then, in 1911, a joint expedition of the National Geographic Society and Yale University found it. Drawn by rumors of a lost city, Professor Hiram Bingham of Yale explored the Peruvian jungle. A single coin worth about 50 cents bought him directions to a hidden trail which he followed up into the thinning air of the great Machu Picchu peak.

There he came upon artificially built walls and steps and at last he climbed into the outer walls and ruins of what was once known as Vitcos, the last stronghold of Manco, the puppet Inca ruler who was set up and later dethroned by Pizarro.

This great lost city covered many acres, with buildings, towers, plazas, rooms, courtyards, and gardens built of what had been the finest stonework. All of its once splendid details had been crumbled by the ages, but even in ruins it still was an awesome sight. Yet there was no trace of the fabulous Inca treasure the Spaniards were after. Somewhere in the Andes there still lie buried the vast hoards of treasure the Incas brought to the hidden city of Machu Picchu.

# Sunken Ships

THE BOTTOM OF THE SEA holds its share of buried treasure. The popular version of a sunken pirate ship is sketched at A, listing a bit to one side, tattered sails moving with the underwater currents, and perhaps a skeleton or two slouching about its decks. In the picture the rigging is still pretty much intact, and although there are a few holes, the ship might be raised and after a bit of repair sent on its way.

In reality, sunken pirate ships are not at all like this. In the first place, all wooden parts would have been eaten away long ago by Teredo shipworms. The rigging would have rotted away and the metal fittings would have broken and sunk to the bottom. Any skeletons would have vanished. Only the heavier metal parts would remain, and the ballast stones would be well covered and concealed with layer upon layer of coral and sand. The sunken ship would look much like the sketch at *B*, merely an uneven spot in the ocean floor, with perhaps a coral-encrusted cannon or two to give away its location. Finding such a wreck is a lot harder than you'd think, and a job for experienced divers.

About the only sign of such a wreck is the fact that it looks a bit "different" from the rest of the ocean debris. If a cannon can be recognized under layers of coral "cement," it is a help, of course. Even metal parts are usually reduced to iron oxide, silver oxide, or copper oxide. Sea water acts as an electrolyte, and when two metals of a different molecular weight are close together, a galvanic current is set up to destroy one of the metals, while the other is saved. If, for example, a silver coin rests against an iron nail, the nail will be punished, but the silver will remain pretty much in its original state. Such materials as pottery and porcelain are not affected by this action, and frequently silver or other metals inside an iron chest will be saved while the chest itself is ruined.

Finding buried treasure, then, is often a matter of knowing what to look for. A valueless piece of coral, for example, as sketched at *C*, may be taken from the site of a wreck. An X-ray may then reveal that it is really a collection of old coins, bar metal, spikes, or perhaps even a pewter tankard. The recovery of such artifacts is a delicate and complicated job. Experts use chemicals to remove the covering, and then fine tools to expose and clean the "hidden" treasure within.

# Black Knight of Canterbury

IT IS COMMONLY BELIEVED that animals, particularly dogs, can sense the presence of ghosts or other supernatural beings where mere humans are not aware of them. Perhaps it is true.

A lady I heard about was visiting a small English town. She had her terrier with her, and it was her custom to take the pup for a walk every afternoon. Since she was a stranger in town, she asked one of the local people where she could walk the dog without losing her way. If she went a certain way, she was told, took a lane to the left and kept left, she would come back to the inn with no trouble at all.

It was gray and misty as she set forth, her dog at her heels, on what she thought would be a pleasant walk. Presently she came to the sunken, grassy lane and started down it in the mist. The little terrier raced ahead, enjoying his freedom to explore.

Suddenly she saw her pet stop short. For a moment he was still, staring ahead into the mist. Then he tucked his tail between his legs, and with his back hair raised and his ears laid back, he raced back to her and hid under her long skirts, trembling and whimpering. She peered intently down the lane but could see nothing. A moment later a strong blast of air struck her and passed on behind her, such as she might have felt if a galloping horse had come thundering by. As she whirled about to peer behind her, the quaking terrier emerged from his hiding place. Still she saw nothing, and presently the dog trotted off down the lane, again unconcerned.

Later, back at the inn, she told of the dog's odd behavior. The innkeeper nodded, neither puzzled nor surprised. She was not the first, he said, to meet the ghost of d'Tracy, one of the four black knights who had murdered Thomas à Becket, Archbishop of Canterbury, in 1170. After the murder, the four knights had raced off in separate directions to avoid capture. D'Tracy, riding at full gallop, had taken the road from Canterbury to Dover, which had once gone through that grassy lane.

Even centuries late, when it was misty and gray, walkers on the lane had felt the rush of wind as the ghostly murderer once more raced past them in headlong flight.

What sight had filled that spunky terrier's heart with panic? Could it be that he had peered back through the ages to see that oncoming horse and its infamous rider? Perhaps it really is true that dogs can see what we cannot.

# The White Dove

MANY YEARS AGO in an Alabama village there lived a man and his wife who were supremely happy together. After years of wedded bliss the wife became very ill, and nothing could be done to save her. Just before she died, she announced to all the family and servants that she would return to the garden in the form of a white dove, so that she could be with her husband where they had known such true love and happiness. Moments later she passed away.

No white dove appeared to make true the dying wife's promise, and the months and years passed by. Eventually the widower fell in love with another woman and decided to marry her and bring her to the big house to live. On the day that he carried his new bride between the white pillars and into the house, a white dove came fluttering into the garden and perched upon a white snowball bush by the gate, where it uttered long, low moans as though it were heartbroken.

Every afternoon it returned to moan and sigh on the snowball bush. The servants were upset and frightened, for sure enough, they thought, the first wife's promise had been carried out at long last. Eventually the second wife heard of the story and she too became disturbed. Soon people came from the village and from neighboring plantations to stare over the garden wall at the dove on the snowball bush. The new wife became more nervous and ill-tempered, and the happy home began to crumble. The husband, frantic, decided upon drastic action, for, legend or no legend, he wanted to preserve his new life.

The next afternoon when the dove appeared he seized his rifle and slipped from the house, stealthily working his way into the garden to where the dove sat moaning and sobbing on the snowball bush. He raised his rifle and fired. A woman's scream answered the blast of the gun and the dove flew away, its breast reddened with blood.

That night as the husband slept, he died. No one could ever determine the cause. His widow moved away. The great house soon fell into ruins, and the yards and garden became a mass of weeds.

The master of the house was buried by the snowball bush, and they say his gravestone is still there, but there are no visitors. No, there is one. For it is said that every spring when the white blossoms of the snowball bush first open, the dove with the red-splotched breast once more appears among them and moans pitifully, recalling the tragic past.

# Gasparilla's Legacy

SOMEWHERE DOWN IN FLORIDA, near St. Augustine, there is a chest buried by an ancient live oak. In it is a small fortune in pirate gold.

In 1785, Gasparilla, the famed pirate, tired of the risks and hardships of his business of piracy, decided to change his ways and become a law-abiding citizen. He planned to leave his pirate headquarters on Gasparilla Island and head for Anastasia Island, just off the coast of St. Augustine, which was then in the hands of the Spaniards.

From there he intended to contact the Spanish governor of St. Augustine, buy the governor's forgiveness, and arrange for sanctuary in that city. Only thus could he escape from his many enemies. But to carry out his plan, it was necessary to get some cash away from his pirate cronies and hide it where he could lay his hands upon it later. This is all recorded in his diary.

He dropped anchor just off Anastasia and, alone, rowed ashore in a small boat. With him was a small chest containing $50,000 in coins. From the ship his henchmen watched him draw the boat onto the beach and stride off into the dense foliage. An hour or so later he returned without the chest and rowed back to the ship.

According to an old document, he went "a short distance inland, turning from the sea marshes into a jungle of palms, sage trees, and live oaks, where I travelled about a half an hour, stopping under a large live oak tree, where I buried a small chest which contained $50,000."

That is the only record of Gasparilla's treasure. The chest of gold may still be there, for the pirate never used it to buy his pardon. A short time after he buried the coins, his ship was seized in Charlotte Harbor and he jumped overboard to his death. He had never returned for the chest and none of his crew knew exactly where the live oak tree was.

By now that tree is probably gone and there may even be a filling station or a beach house where it stood. It's too bad that Gasparilla couldn't have been a bit more specific with his directions.

# The Sealed Cave

EVERY SO OFTEN an old Indian who lived far back in the New Mexico mountains with his wife and son came into town with a small bar of gold. Each bar was marked with Spanish symbols. Since it is illegal for an individual to possess such gold bars, they were confiscated each time. However, the Indian kept persevering. After a while he finally revealed that the bars came from a cave in the mountains, but he refused to tell exactly where the cave was. In addition to the gold, he said, he could see through a small opening that there was far more treasure in the cave, as well as swords, armor, and other relics of what might have been a Spanish expedition of long ago. All attempts to spy upon him were foiled.

It wasn't long after the Indian told this story that his trips to town stopped. Nobody saw him for many months. Then one day he returned, but he didn't have any gold with him. Asked what had happened, he related how his wife and son were eager to get all the treasure. They had urged him to open the cave to make access easy, but he refused. And so they decided to do it themselves, as soon as they had the opportunity.

His son had obtained some explosives and hid them until the old man was to be away. Then he and his mother could enlarge the opening to the inner cave, which had closed up over the years by the shifting of the rocks in the cavern.

As soon as the man left, his wife and son set about their project with enthusiasm. But they had too much enthusiasm — and too much powder — for when the explosive charge went off, it worked in complete reverse. The explosion brought down most of the interior, sealing not only the treasure-filled inner room but the outer cave too, where the gold bars were hidden. The entire cavern was buried under tons and tons of rock and earth, forever sealing the treasure within the mountains.

# The Señora of Cottage Gardens

In Natchez, Mississippi, it is said, the ghost of a young and beautiful lady still wanders among the magnolias of Cottage Gardens.

It all began many years ago, long before the Civil War, at a time when Spain owned that part of the country, and a Spanish representative, Don José Vidal, was governor.

Don José lived in a low rambling white mansion of heavy timbers, surrounded by magnolias and catalpa trees, unlike the huge double-galleried homes built later.

While he was acting as governor for his country he sailed home to Spain and returned with a lovely young bride to be with him in this foreign land. She was small and delicate, with great charm and dignity, and soon she made many friends. Cottage Gardens was the scene of many a gay party in the months to come.

Hardly two years had passed when a frightful epidemic of yellow fever struck almost overnight. All of Natchez was ravaged by the dread plague. Not even the governor's lady was spared, in her room above the magnolias. She too came down with the fever and soon knew that she would die, for in those days nothing could be done for the sufferers. She also knew that the plague victims were buried as quickly as possible, so

117

there would be no time for a fine funeral. Her request was that she be buried on the high bluffs overlooking the Mississippi River she had grown to love.

When the end came, she was laid to rest in a hastily erected brick vault on the bluffs. The governor then fled across the river to be safe from the plague running rampant over the land. From his haven he could see the tiny vault high on the cliff, and every night he prayed for the soul of his young bride.

Ever since then, people have said that the gardens of what was once the governor's mansion have been haunted by the ghost of the governor's lady. During the Civil War, soldiers who were billeted in Natchez claimed that they saw a flitting female figure among the magnolias — a figure that refused to halt to challenge, and eluded pursuit like a phantom.

Persons passing on the Kings Highway close by often reported seeing the figure, and even today many claim to have seen the doña's ghost flitting about the shady gardens. Even those who do not believe in ghosts wonder why, at certain times, dogs whine and slink behind their masters' legs when passing the old house. Could they alone see the pale and beautiful hostess of Cottage Gardens roaming about?

It is said that when she appears, her dimly glowing figure is followed by a faint melody not unlike that from a guitar. It is said, too, that the melody is foreign, sad, and with a Spanish rhythm. Perhaps the ghost of Don José has returned as well, to keep his phantom bride company among the moonlit shadows under the magnolias along the Mississippi.

# Card Game at Buxton Inn

ON A COLD AND STORMY NIGHT around the turn of the century, the patrons of the Buxton Inn in Maine were sitting around the roaring fire in the taproom swapping yarns and drinking a warming brew. Suddenly there was a loud, insistent knocking at the door.

The innkeeper hurried to open it and a young man entered. His rich clothes were trimmed with gold lace and he carried a cape over his arm. He shook the snow from his tall beaver hat, stamped his booted feet, and strode to the fireplace.

The others looked up with interest, admiring his fine attire, but also noting that it was somewhat old-fashioned and unusual for the area. Undoubtedly, they thought, he was a traveller from some distant city. One of them offered him a place close to the crackling hearth, and suggested that he join them in a game of cards. With a cheerful smile he agreed.

As the evening and the game progressed, the young man had uncanny good luck with every deal of the cards. The other players all felt that there was something familiar about the handsome young man, as though they had seen him many times before but couldn't place him. Oddly enough, he knew many of them by name, but never introduced himself.

It was nearly morning when another patron entered.

As he removed his greatcoat and boots, he called to the innkeeper. "I say, what's happened to your sign? I thought I must have the wrong tavern."

The others looked up in startled surprise, then rushed to the window to see the swinging sign outside the door. Wiping the steam from the glass, they saw with astonishment that there was nothing upon the sign but the words "Buxton Inn." The center was blank. Then they knew.

With wonder and fright upon their rugged faces they turned once more to the fireplace, but the dapper young card expert was gone, leaving nothing but a small puddle of melted snow beneath the chair where his boots had rested. No wonder he had looked familiar.

Almost fearfully they turned again to look at the tavern's sign. It must have been a trick of the storm, for now, as clearly as ever, they could see the painting of young Sir Charles, resplendent in his tall beaver hat and flowing cape, as he had stood for many years. Then something else caught their eye — something they had never noticed before. One of the pockets of his breeches seemed to be bulging as though with many coins, and a smile played about the painted mouth — the kind of smile a young man wears when he has been lucky at cards.

# The Horse with the Braids

EVERY PART OF THE COUNTRY has its share of tales about witches, ghosts, and supernatural happenings. This one comes from upstate New York, where a farmer lived with his wife and elderly mother.

After years of living a peaceful and normal life on his prosperous farm, the farmer noticed one morning that his old gray mare seemed exhausted, as though she had been running all night. Something else was strange too: her mane and tail were neatly braided. The next morning — and the next — he found the mare in the same condition. Nobody in his right mind, he knew, would work a horse all night, and who would bother to braid her mane and tail? The farmer's bewilderment increased, and he told his wife and old mother about the extraordinary situation. They were frightened, and talked of witches. His mother was particularly worried and begged him to let things alone. It was risky, she insisted, to interfere with the supernatural. He finally said he'd let things go on as they were for a while, as long as the mare wasn't too tired to work in the fields the next day.

And so it continued for several weeks — each morning the horse was tired, and each morning her mane and tail were neatly braided.

One night, shortly after midnight, the farmer had

to get something from the stable. As he entered, his lantern held high, he was startled to see a huge jet black cat sitting upon the horse's back. The horse was trembling as though in panic, and her mane and tail were neatly braided.

In a rage, the farmer seized a handy pitchfork and rushed at the cat, jabbing its back with the three sharp tines as it leaped away. The horse whinnied, and as the farmer calmed the animal, he was astonished to see the mane and tail slowly unbraid themselves and hang naturally again.

Considerably shaken by his experience, he hurried back to the house and slipped into bed, filled with terror at what he had witnessed.

The next morning he hurriedly dressed and rushed downstairs to tell his wife and mother about the night's adventure. But his mother refused to leave her room, claiming she was ill. A doctor was finally called. Over her violent objections, he examined her — and found three puncture wounds in her back. The wounds never healed, but remained open and sore until the old woman's death some months later. She refused to tell how she got them, but the horrified son and his wife knew very well indeed. For it was she who had been sitting upon the mare's back that wild night, in the form of a black cat.

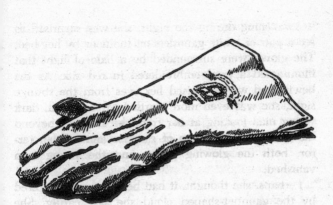

# The Gauntlet in the Castle

WHILE SIGHT-SEEING IN SCOTLAND, a young American lady joined a group that was visiting an island where a crumbling castle had recently been opened to the public. As they approached the castle, the young lady noticed that a huge cloud overhead looked like a pair of gauntlets. She called it to the attention of the others in the party, but thought no more about it. The unusual cloud formation soon faded away.

Later that day a sudden and violent storm came up. Because the trip back to the mainland was too rough for their small boat, the sight-seers were forced to spend the night at the castle. The young American was given a room in one of the towers, and she went to bed quite thrilled over the unexpected chance to spend a night there.

123

Awakening during the night, she was surprised to see a pair of white gauntlets on the floor by her bed. The gloves were surrounded by a halo of light that illuminated a crest embroidered in red silk. As the bewildered woman raised her eyes from the strange sight, she was even more startled to see a tall, dark young man looking at her from the shadows beyond the gloves. At her gasp of surprise and sudden terror, both the glowing gloves and the young man vanished.

Perhaps, she thought, it had been a dream inspired by the gauntlet-shaped cloud she saw earlier. She didn't mention her ghostly visitor to anyone.

Several years passed. In New York, she met a young Scotsman and married him. Shortly after their honeymoon, he received word that a maiden aunt had died in New England, and the newlyweds had to go there to close the house. It was very run down and dilapidated, with hardly a sign that it had been lived in. The young bride occupied herself by poking about the attic. There in an old trunk, neatly wrapped in a bit of tartan, was a pair of gauntlet gloves, exactly the same as those she had seen in the castle years before.

She hurried downstairs in excitement to show them to her husband and tell him about the strange coincidence. When she held them out to him, he turned deathly pale. "So, my dear," he said, "you were the girl in the bed that night!" Then he vanished — for the second time. His bride fainted, and when she came to she was alone. Even the furniture had disappeared. Questioning the neighbors later, she was told that no one had lived there for a hundred years.

# Great Wheel of Light

THE SEAS ARE A MYSTERIOUS AND STRANGE WORLD unto themselves, and many things happen upon their surfaces and beneath their waves which mere man has difficulty explaining away. Phantom ships, sea serpents, mysterious sounds and lights all seem ridiculous to those who did not witness them. But to those who encounter such unusual phenomena they are very real indeed.

So real are they that they are sometimes recorded in ships' logs, set down in the matter-of-fact language of seafaring men. Such an entry was made on June 10, 1909, in the log of the Danish steamship *Bintang*.

As the *Bintang* was steaming through the night in the Straits of Malacca, between Sumatra and the Malay Peninsula, the captain was astonished to see what appeared to be a long beam of light under the water. Like the beam of a searchlight, it seemed to be sweeping across the floor of the sea. The beam passed across the sea before him and was followed by another and then another, like the revolving spokes of a wheel, or searchlight beams following one another across the sky.

Soon, some distance from the ship, there appeared a brighter spot or hub, from which the long beams of underwater light seemed to stem. The beams revolved silently as the rotating "wheel" slowly approached the *Bintang*. In the words of the captain, "Long arms issued from a center around which the whole system appeared to rotate."

The great revolving wheel was so huge that only half of it could be seen above the horizon. As it revolved toward the *Bintang*, the crew stared in dumfounded amazement. Looking around, they realized that the long arms of light could not possibly be a reflection of their own lights, and there was no other ship in sight.

As the great silent revolving wheel of underwater light came nearer, it seemed to sink lower into the water and grow dimmer and dimmer. Finally it vanished deep beneath the waves and the Straits of Malacca were once more black and empty.

No one knows what it was the bewildered men saw that night, although the record of the strange encounter has been published by the Danish Meteorological Institute, an organization not given to publishing anything but well-documented material.

# Ruby Cat

A FAMOUS JEWEL THIEF who was known by the name of Klaus Gudden arrived in Germany in 1894. He had with him two fabulous matched rubies. The jewels had originally been the eye of a statue in a Korean temple. That was in about 165 A.D. Then they were stolen from the statue. In 1560 they were acquired by the Sultan of the Ottoman Empire. He in turn gave them to a lady. The rubies cost her her life, for a thief killed her to get them. Later they belonged to Louis XV, who gave them to Madame Pompadour. She eventually sold them to a Russian nobleman. How Gudden came by them will probably never be known.

In any event, as soon as he appeared in Berlin, the police began searching for him. He was caught and, as he tried to escape, he was shot and killed. But the

127

jewels were not found. A few years later, a gem expert named Graves attempted to find out what happened to them, for they couldn't vanish into thin air. Undoubtedly Gudden had hidden them on the chance that he could return for them later.

Mr. Graves learned that when the police set their dragnet, Gudden was trapped in a certain block in Berlin. He had been unable to leave that block for several days. Searching for clues in that limited area, Graves discovered that Gudden had visited a little ceramic shop on the very day that he had been killed.

This shop specialized in clay cats, and Gudden had picked up one that had just been removed from the kiln. After looking it over for several minutes, he asked the owner to set that cat aside for him until he returned for it. He scratched an "X" on the bottom and left orders not to sell it to anyone else.

Sometime later when the shop owner learned that his strange customer had been killed, he included the cat in a shipment with dozens of others just like it.

Graves traced the shipment to America, but there the trail branched out into a hundred directions. The cats had been sold all over the country and it was impossible to trace them all.

Somewhere one of those cats may hold within its clay body a half-million dollars in rubies. Eight inches high, it lies in a reclining position with its tail wrapped around its body and forepaws. It was originally yellow, but by now it must be darker and cracked and chipped with age. The faint "X" on the bottom may no longer be visible, but the years will not have damaged the fortune it guards.

# Haunted Schoolhouse

THE SMALL SCHOOLHOUSE in Newburyport, Massachusetts, was the scene of a strange phenomenon in 1870. Every day a mysterious yellow glow spread over the classroom, windows, and blackboards. It usually started near the hall door and spread silently over the room. After about two minutes it faded away. It did no harm while it cast its light over the room, but afterward the students and the teacher, Miss Lucy A. Perkins, felt weak and ill.

The yellow radiance was not the only unusual occurrence. There was also a breeze of cold air that swept through the room, even when the doors and windows were tightly closed. The chill breeze rustled the papers, swung the faded map on the wall and shook the hanging lamp. This too, made the teacher and children feel slightly ill, but they kept on with their studies day after day, trying bravely to ignore the strange event.

In the late fall the yellow light disappeared and a low-pitched laugh began to be heard occasionally. One day many of the students, and Miss Lucy, saw a child's hand floating in the air. Then the arm became visible. The climax came on November 1.

During a geography lesson, Miss Lucy called upon a student to recite. In the midst of a sentence he suddenly stopped and pointed to the vestibule. There stood a boy with his arm upraised. It was the same arm and hand that had floated in the air.

The boy stood silently, his arm up and his face and jaw bound in a white cloth as though he had an injured jaw or a toothache. Then, as they all watched, he slowly vanished. From that time on, the schoolhouse was plagued no more.

Three local boys with a reputation for mischief were questioned in an attempt to solve the mystery, but the authorities decided they had had no part in the events. To this day the yellow glow, the cold breeze, and the boy with the upraised arm and bandaged jaw have never been explained.

# The Man Who Fell Forever

CURLY WAS A SAILOR who was fascinated by high places. No mast was too tall for him to ascend, no cliff too sheer for him to peer over and no tower too shaky for him to climb. He frequently talked of what a wonderful sensation it must be to fall from a great height.

When his ship dropped anchor at a South American port, Curly was determined to climb an old abandoned stone lighthouse. His friends argued that he couldn't get to the top, and bets were placed on Curly's success. Another sailor was designated to go with him to act as a witness. And so the two entered the musty, damp old tower and started up the crumbling stairway.

When they emerged on the balcony far above the sand dunes, they tried to attract the attention of the group below. But their shouts did not carry to the men, who were playing cards directly beneath them. Curly's companion finally tied his jacknife in his handkerchief, Curly put in his lucky coin for added weight, and they tossed the little bundle over the rusty iron railings of the beacon platform. They lost sight of it as it fell to the depths below, and decided to start back down. Curly seemed to hesitate a moment. Then with a queer grin he said, "I know a quicker way!" and hurled himself over the old railing, plummeting directly down toward the group below.

The other man screamed a warning and then rushed down the stairs, fearful of what he would find when he reached the bottom. He burst out the old doorway, hoping that nobody else had been hurt by Curly's leap. To his astonishment, the rest of the group were still playing cards, as though nothing had hurtled down upon them from the tower above. And nothing had. Curly hadn't landed!

The group searched the ground for yards around, combing the tower, the dunes, and the water below them, but Curly was never seen again. They did find the tied and knotted handkerchief containing the jacknife, but Curly's lucky coin was no longer with it. Perhaps that too, like Curly, had vanished on the way down.

# The Bottled Ghost

SOME GHOSTS seem to have no explanation at all; others frighten people for years, and then suddenly. . . .

Take, for example, one particular house that everyone in town thought was haunted. Many folks who had been near it had heard ghostly moanings and groanings from inside — not just imagined noises but weird sounds that sent chills up the spine and curled the hair.

Occasionally a few daring young boys would sneak a few feet inside the crumbling old doorway, trying to be very brave but secretly hoping they would see and hear nothing to destroy their bravado. Occasionally they did hear low moans from the upper part of the house — and immediately they had urgent business back home. This went on for some time, until finally some of the boys marshalled their courage and decided they might as well take the spook by the sheet, so to speak, and settle it once and for all.

They organized a ghost-hunting party to explore the old house from top to bottom and in between, in search of the source of such mournful sounds, human or otherwise.

With pounding pulses they entered the haunted house. They made their way warily through all the downstairs rooms, and found nothing. Then they worked their way up the creaking stairway to the second floor and inspected the bare, dust-covered rooms there. Only cobwebs, squeaking doors, and rattling windows met their gaze.

The attic was next, and the fear the youngsters felt when they first entered the house was as nothing compared to their feelings as they mounted that last short stairway. But of course none of them could confess to anxiety.

When the dingy attic disclosed nothing, their relief was great. An occasional banging shutter signalled a rising wind, but there was no sign of the ghost they dreaded finding. Suddenly, a soft low moan seemed to fill the empty room. It rose and fell softly, eerily. The young adventurers peered about, trembling. Then they spotted the source of the unearthly sound.

There, stuck in the wall of the attic to seal a knocked-out knothole, was a dusty old bottle. Its neck stuck clear through to the outside where the rising wind could blow across it. The higher the wind, the louder the ghostly moans.

And so the bottled ghost was laid to rest, and one more haunted house gave up its secret.

# Hessian Booty

SINCE THE DAYS of America's War of Independence
many people have sought the famous Hessian treasure,
believed to lie somewhere in Massachusetts. It all began shortly after the defeat of General Burgoyne at
Saratoga. Among the British general's troops were
many hired Hessian soldiers who were more interested in looting and plundering the land than in fighting. Indeed, service in the army for many of them
was merely an opportunity to ransack the towns they
passed through. Over the months of fighting, they
had accumulated quite a hoard of valuables.

After Burgoyne's defeat, many of these hired Hessians fled eastward in the general direction of Boston,
carrying their stolen treasure. In addition to their
small arms, they had several small cannons with them.

News of their flight raced on ahead of them, and in
Massachusetts a band of angry colonials was hastily

organized to try and stop them before they could reach Boston. From a small band of farmers, the pursuing force grew until it was thought large enough to stand against the veteran Hessians. The spot picked for the battle was near Dalton, in the western part of Massachusetts.

As the Hessians began to find their flight impeded by more and more rifle fire from the hills about them, they decided to take a stand and fight it out with the farmer-soldiers who were attacking from all sides along their route.

It soon became evident, however, that the Hessians had met their match and were fighting a losing battle. What could they do with their plundered loot? The only answer was to bury it, they decided, in the hope that some day, when the war was over, they could recover it.

Under cover of darkness, according to one story, the money and jewels were stuffed into the cannon barrels and buried on the spot. Then the angry colonials closed in.

After the battle was over, the few Hessians who remained alive did not know exactly where the booty had been buried. That was almost two centuries ago, and since then many hundreds of folks have tried to find the lost Hessian treasure buried in the barrels of iron cannons somewhere in the hills about Dalton. Perhaps some unsuspecting hunter has eaten his lunch right over the spot where the rusted cannons still guard the stolen treasure.

# The Man in the Golden Armor

GHOSTLY ARMIES, phantom warriors, and mysterious visions during battles have been part of our unsolved legends through the ages. Such incidents never cease to intrigue and mystify even the skeptics. Take, for example, the case of "the man in the golden armor," seen on August 28, 1914, during a battle of World War I.

Scores of soldiers reported this incident and one person in particular heard it many times. This was an English nurse, Miss Phyllis Campbell, who first heard the story from a wounded soldier of the Royal Field Artillery.

In a hospital behind the lines, he spoke of the battle, As his unit defended a hill, he said, it looked as if the whole German army were attacking at once. Just as he was about to give up in despair, it happened. A cloud of light appeared ahead of the swarming Germans as their horses charged up the slope. Then the light cleared away and revealed the figure of a tall man with yellow hair and golden armor, astride a white horse. The man's uplifted arm held a mighty sword.

As the R.F.A. man watched in astonishment, the attacking Germans, halted, turned, and raced back down the hill just as victory was at their lance tips. At once

137

the British were after them, and no one seemed to know what had happened to "the man in the golden armor" or when he had vanished.

Nurse Campbell later heard this story from other wounded men who had been in the same sector of the front. All told the same story, with simple conviction. But what about the story from the other side, the German side? Phyllis Campbell had the unique experience of hearing that too.

A German nurse who had been a friend of hers before the war served in a hospital in Potsdam. A month or so after the British soldiers told Miss Campbell the story about the figure on the white charger, she received a letter from her friend in Germany. In it there was a question about stories going around the German hospital. A regiment that had been assigned to capture a certain hill had failed to do so. The German officers reported that, as they attacked, there were suddenly strange shapes in the sky and then a huge man on a white horse appeared. Their charging horses had turned and fled, disregarding all commands and obstacles in their headlong terror-stricken flight. It had been impossible to stop or turn them back up the hill.

The German nurse concluded her letter with the simple query: "That is the way they talk. Is there something to it, Phyllis?" Who could answer that with certainty?

# No Grass on the Grave

IN 1821, JOHN NEWTON, a Welshman, was sentenced to death by hanging for a crime he stoutly maintained he did not commit. All through his long and controversial trial he continued to insist upon his innocence, but the two main witnesses against him were prominent citizens of the town, and their word carried more weight than his.

They were unwavering in their accusations against him, for if John Newton were acquitted, suspicion would fall on them. Their stories were long and loud, and at last the court was convinced of his guilt.

As the death sentence was passed on him, Newton turned to the judge and jury and said quietly, "I am innocent, and no grass will grow over my grave for a generation to prove it."

In due time he was hanged, and his body was

buried in the local churchyard. Although no one really believed what he had said, the sod was replaced with special care. In a matter of days, however, the newly replaced sod turned brown and died. Not only did the grass over his grave wither, but the bare spot of earth was in the shape of his coffin. The townspeople, disturbed over what they considered a mere coincidence, promptly replaced the sod, only to have the new grass die for no apparent reason.

Several attempts were made to break the curse of John Newton. Fresh soil was put over his grave and special grass seed planted there, but to no avail. The bare spot remained mute testimony to his innocence.

In 1852, an article about the incident was published. "Thirty years have passed," it said, "and the grass has not covered John Newton's grave."

This account rekindled interest in the case, and a new attempt was made to fill in the rectangular area. Fresh sod was brought to the churchyard and carefully set into place. Soon the grass over the head of the grave died as before, but for some time the rest of the area was partially covered with the new growth. However, a few months later that too withered, and once again the accusing coffin shape appeared. In 1886, more than a generation after John Newton was hanged, the spot was still bare, but then a change began to be noticed.

Grass started to grow on the sides and fill in the area. The grassy spot gradually took a new shape. The grave was never completely covered, but by 1941 the grass upon it had assumed the shape of a cross.

# The Frightened Dog

A FADED PHOTOGRAPH I've had for many years shows
a tall, thin boy and a white dog sitting on a porch.
Tom, the boy in the picture, grew up in North Carolina, where he and his friends often went on hunting
trips into the woods and swamps.

One day they set forth with their guns and Tom's
dog, planning to be gone only a few hours. However,
late that afternoon it began to rain very hard. Since
they were far from home, they decided to spend the
night in an abandoned shack they had stumbled upon,
rather than try to find their way home in the dark.
The shack was empty except for some rubbish, a few
old clothes, and a lantern which still had some kero-
sene it it. Eventually the boys fell asleep on the floor,
with the dog curled up beside them, while the rain
splattered upon the roof overhead.

Some time during the night the boys were awakened
by the dog whining and scratching at the door to get
out. They noticed that he was trembling violently, and
that the hair on his back was raised as though he were
either frightened or angry.

Rather sleepily, one of the boys started for the door
to let the pup out. Then he froze in his tracks, From
the black woods outside the shack came a weird,
startling sound. A combination of whine, low moan,

and rising and falling wail, it was like nothing the boys had heard before anywhere. They all stared at each other, and reached for their light rifles for protection, as the dog ran about the shack, barking and whining and showing his teeth. One boy quickly lighted the lantern.

The window openings of the shack contained no glass but were covered with mosquito netting, and suddenly the dog hurled himself through one of these opening and ran off into the woods, snarling and barking.

The three boys waited with hearts pounding and .22's clutched in their hands. The strange sound from outside faded away in the distance and then there was nothing but the patter of rain on the tin roof to break the silence.

A few minutes later the boys heard running footsteps outside. Before they could raise their guns, the dog leaped back through the broken netting and came toward them, whining and shaking, with his tail tucked between his legs. He was a very frightened white dog. That was the most amazing part of the adventure, for when he had left the shack to run into the woods after the "thing," he had been black!

# Unexpected Trip

HAVE YOU EVER FOUND YOURSELF unable to resist an impulse that you couldn't explain? The lady who had this eerie adventure was helpless to resist it, and still cannot understand why and how it happened.

She had been in New York for the day and was ready to return to her suburban home. When she arrived at Grand Central Station to catch her train, she noticed that the *Twilight Limited* for Springfield, Massachusetts, was ready to leave and passengers were going down the ramp to get aboard.

Her father lived in a small town a few miles outside Springfield, and many times in the past she had taken that very train to visit him. Tonight she had no intention of going there, but nevertheless she found herself walking down the ramp to the Springfield-bound express. She seemed, somehow, totally unable to stop herself as she boarded the train.

Seating herself, she thought that it was all perfectly ridiculous; yet she made no effort to get off. It all seemed part of a prearranged plan that she should be there instead of on her own train heading home. She counted her money and saw that she had enough to buy a ticket to her father's home. Then she settled back to make the trip, giving no thought to her family's reaction to her absence.

As the train sped away from New York, she wondered why this had all happened. Why had it seemed like the right thing — the important thing — to do instead of going home? She was a grown woman, with responsibilities, and yet there she was, speeding into the night to a destination far away.

When the train arrived at Springfield, she alighted and took the bus to the town where her father lived alone since the death of his wife some years before. When she reached the house, it was completely dark, but she tried the front door and to her surprise found it unlocked.

She entered and turned on the lights. There seemed to be no one there, but presently her father's voice called feebly from upstairs, "Is that you?" He called her by name. She tossed aside her packages and hurried up the familiar stairs to his room, snapping on the light by the door. Now she knew the reason for the unexpected trip to her father's house. He was in bed, seriously ill, and completely unable to call for help from outside or even reach the light switch by himself.

Later, when she asked him why he had called her name as she had entered the darkened house after her strange urge to travel there from New York, he merely smiled and said very simply, "Why, I knew you were coming."

# Lake of Gold

IF YOU WERE TOLD where someone had thrown a vast treasure, you might assume that it would be a simple matter to rush right over and pick it up. It's not always that easy, even when you know just where it is. This is the situation in Lake Guatavita, high in the Cordillera Mountains of Colombia, one of the greatest treasure-trove areas in all the world.

This lake, 10,000 feet up in the mountains north of Santa Fe de Bogotá, was for centuries the scene of wild ceremonies when chiefs were crowned or religious observances took place. As part of the ritual, when a new Inca chief was appointed he gilded him-

145

self with a coating of pure gold dust and plunged under the sacred water of the lake.

In connection with such ceremonies, the natives threw vast quantities of gold, jewels, and other valuables into the waters from the shore. At other times, to appease various gods whole villages gathered their valuables, marched to the lake shore and threw their treasures into the water. Once, to foil a Spanish invader, the chief of the Chibcha tribe threw more than two tons of gold into the lake. In all, it is estimated that almost six billion dollars' worth of treasure is at the bottom of Lake Guatavita.

Yet all the many attempts to reach this vast hoard have failed to turn up more than a few small gold images, jewels, and coins.

Why? In the first place, the lake is a thousand feet wide at its narrowest point, and reaches a depth of more than a thousand feet. At its shallowest part, it is still nearly fifty feet deep, and no one knows exactly where the treasure was thrown from the shore. Over the ages, layer upon layer of sediment, rotten vegetation, and mud has settled over the vast treasure below the surface.

One English salvage company did attempt to retrieve a part of the great fortune from the bottom, but only recovered a few hundred dollars' worth to pay for the great expense of their expedition to the site. According to reports, it would take a vast amount of machinery, diving equipment, and money even to begin an effective salvage operation.

146

# The Doctor's Visitor

DR. S. WEIR MITCHELL of Philadelphia was one of the nation's foremost neurologists during the latter part of the 19th century. One snowy evening, after a particularly hard day, he retired early, and was just falling asleep when his doorbell rang loudly. He hoped it had been a trick of his ears or that his caller would go away, but the bell rang again even more insistently. Struggling awake, he snatched a robe and stumbled down to see who it was. He muttered in annoyance as he slid the bolt to unlock the door, completely unprepared for the shivering child who stood there in the swirling snow.

The small pale girl trembled on the doorstep, for a thin frock and a ragged shawl were her only protection against the blustering snow-filled wind. For a moment they stared at each other. Then she said in a small, plaintive voice, "My mother is very sick — won't you come, please?"

Dr. Mitchell explained that he had retired for the night and suggested that the child call another doctor in the neighborhood. But she wouldn't leave and, looking up at him with her tear-filled eyes, pleaded again, "Won't you come, *please?*" No one — and certainly no doctor — could refuse this pitiful appeal.

With a resigned sigh, thinking longingly of his

warm bed, the physician asked the child to step inside while he hurriedly dressed and picked up his bag. The child then gestured for him to follow her out into the storm.

In a house several streets away he found a woman desperately sick with pneumonia. He recognized her immediately as someone who had once worked for him as a servant, and he bent over the bed, determined to save her. As he worked, the doctor complimented her on her daughter's fortitude and persistence in getting him there.

The woman stared unbelievingly at the doctor for a moment, and then said in a weak whisper, "That is impossible. My little girl died more than a month ago. Her dress is still hanging in that cupboard over there!"

With strange emotions Dr. Mitchell strode to the cupboard and opened it. Inside were hanging the little dress and the tattered shawl that his caller had worn. They were warm and dry, and could never have been out in the storm!

# Women in White

Men who spend much of their lives at sea are full of tales of ghosts, premonitions, haunted ships, and strange apparitions.

Take, for example, the strange dream of the women in white in the rain that plagued John Nelson, the cook aboard the schooner *Sachem*, out of Gloucester. The *Sachem*, under the command of Captain J. Wenzell, had been fishing along Brown's Bank. On September 7, 1871, she pulled her hook and sailed for George's Bank to try for better luck.

That night, as recorded in the log and journal of Captain Wenzell, John Nelson hurried aft to talk to the captain. He was greatly agitated and apparently in mortal fear.

He told the captain that he had just awakened

149

from a dream that he had had twice before in his life — a dream that had been followed both times by shipwreck and tragedy. When the captain asked him to explain, Nelson said that he had dreamed of women, dressed all in white, standing in the rain as though waiting for their men to come back, perhaps from the sea. The cook then begged the captain to head for port or at least to get away from the dangerous George's Bank, noted for storms and reefs.

The captain made little of his fears and urged him to go back to his galley and prepare the evening meal. Mumbling that it would be fatal to stay there after the warning of the "women all in white," Nelson left.

Later in the night it began to blow, and about 1:30 one of the men in the forecastle reported in alarm that the *Sachem* was taking in water. Captain Wenzell hurried below and found six inches of water already sloshing in the hold of the schooner. He quickly ordered that the pumps be manned and a bucket brigade be formed to empty the ship, but, despite their efforts, they could not keep ahead of the in-rushing water. The cook was ordered to provision a lifeboat and be ready to leave if necessary.

Believing that the leak might be on the other side, the captain tacked the schooner in the other direction in an attempt to bring the leak above the waterline. This didn't help. In desperation they signaled another schooner, the *Pescador*. At great risk, the ships were brought together and the men of the doomed schooner were taken off. Shortly after, the *Sachem* rolled over on her side and then slid below the waves, bow first. Once more the "women in white" had been right!

# The Whistle

ON A SMALL ISOLATED FARM in South Carolina an old woman lived alone with her dog. One night, as she was going about her chores, she became conscious of an odd whistling sound somewhere outside. It seemed to surround the house but did not sound like high wind in the pines, noises of nature, or a human whistle. It was very strange. Curious, she went to the farmhouse door. As she did, she noticed that her small terrier was barking and howling on the back porch. This porch, which was enclosed, made a dark and snug haven for the pup.

She opened the door. The wavering and high-pitched whistle seemed to be coming toward the house from across the hills, yet it was as hard to locate as the chirp of a cricket. It must be some of the local youngsters trying to frighten her, she thought, but shut and bolted the door and hastily got her late husband's revolver — just in case. She returned to the door to await whatever might be going to happen next. The dog stayed on the porch, for if it were just pranksters his barking would frighten them away.

The whistle came nearer, although the old woman could see nothing. Then it seemed to turn, pass slowly around the house, and approach the porch, where the now hysterical terrier was almost beside himself with excitement.

Soon there was a terrific outcry and sounds of struggle on the back porch. Then silence — as complete as it was terrifying. The lady, alone in the stillness, shook with fright. She did not dare go out onto the porch. Eventually she went to bed.

The next morning she investigated. The dog was gone, and blood was spattered all about. What had taken place? The whistle had stopped when the struggle began. But what was it that had caused the bloodshed? What happened to the little terrier? Nobody ever found out.

# St. Elmo's Fire

SAILORS, FOR THE MOST PART, are a superstitious lot. Unusual happenings and things they see about their ships and on the water often take on supernatural meaning, even when they have perfectly logical explanations. Every so often an unusual chain of events will strengthen those irrational beliefs.

St. Elmo's Fire, a weird flickering light that is occasionally seen about masts, rigging, and hulls of sailing ships — even the modern ships of today — has long been said to be the sign that St. Elmo was near. The patron saint of sailors is said to have "hoisted his colors over a ship he is protecting" when the queer balls and streamers of light begin to appear about the boat.

In reality, this static electricity, which collects near metal parts of a ship under certain conditions, has no more to do with protection than the baby's shoes some motorists dangle from the windshield, but once in a while events seem to prove otherwise.

In 1873, during a terrific storm off the Queero fishing banks, the captain of one vessel sighted a wrecked ship, buffeted by the storm and apparently on fire. The captain identified her as a French ship from Brittany and called one of his own crew, a Frenchman, from below to see the wreck. The sailor took one look at the pitching wreck with the fire about its hull and burst out laughing. The other men were amazed. What manner of man was he, to laugh at the plight of some of his own countrymen aboard a doomed and blazing ship?

The Frenchman explained his lack of concern. The ship, he said, was perfectly safe in spite of the terrible storm and the loss of all its masts and rigging, for the "fire" was the sign that the patron saint of all sailors, St. Elmo, had taken charge and would see them safely through the storm. But the other men were convinced that there wasn't one chance in a thousand that the wreck would stay afloat during the storm. Even their own ship, in perfect condition, was in danger. No, the wallowing French wreck could not possibly last out the storm, and was soon lost to sight in the rain and high seas.

Yet the following night the wreck was sighted again and the crew were taken off, battered but safe. All 18 men were rescued from the drifting wreck. Had they been worried or panic-stricken by their plight during the storm?

"Of course not," the French sailors replied. "With St. Elmo in charge, and his colors flying along our hull and rigging, how could we be in any danger?"

Of such "miracles" are the legends and superstitions of the sea made. Perhaps science, with its logical explanations, isn't always as convincing as the simple beliefs of a seaman.

154

# Clear-sky Showers

IN TROPICAL COUNTRIES there are small and very clearly defined showers which are limited to a small area only. In Puerto Rico, I have seen such small wandering showers going past in the sugar-cane fields, or encountered them in villages where it rained on only one side of the street.

Some showers occur when the sun is shining overhead and there is not a cloud visible anywhere. Scientists are not sure just what causes these "clear-sky showers."

In October, 1886, in Charlotte, North Carolina, such showers came. Every afternoon about three o'clock rain fell in one small area, between two tall trees. Sometimes it was sunny, sometimes cloudy, but still the rain fell. If the shower were heavy, it covered about a half acre of land; if it were slight, it fell only between the two trees. The trees were always the center of the rain that fell straight down. Hundreds of people, several trained in meteorology, witnessed the phenomenon, but none could explain it.

A month earlier a similar occurrence took place in Dawson, Georgia. Rain fell from a clear and cloudless sky in an area of only 25 square feet. During the shower, the sun was shining brightly.

At about the same time, it was reported that similar

restricted showers had fallen in even smaller areas in South Carolina. In one instance an area only about 10 feet square was affected, as though someone had poured a bucket of water on the spot from high in the air.

What made the rainfall in Charlotte so perplexing was the fact that it came every afternoon for several weeks at the same time, in the same place.

The following year, a similar localized fall was reported in Geneva, Switzerland, in the month of August. This time, the water was warm. Perhaps the Swiss prefer hot to cold showers.

# Tragedy Atop the Glacier

IN THIS DAY OF FLIGHTS over long stretches of water, uncharted jungles, and polar wastes it is small wonder that occasionally an aircraft and its passengers are lost forever. Usually some evidence is recovered to settle the fate of the passengers, but sometimes the tragedy has an unexplained and bewildering twist.

The Curtiss C-46 *Commando,* sometimes referred to as *Dumbo,* was a huge aircraft that did very well with its two engines and was able to carry along with one if necessary. It had two floors, the upper for passengers and the lower for baggage, cargo, or extra fuel in special tanks. It was a rugged ship, and it took many men and supplies to their destination safely and quickly during World War II.

One of those efficient C-46's carried 32 men, most of them members of the military services, on a flight over the state of Washington. Although the weather was bad, the flight was routine. After the plane passed a mountainous section of the state southeast of Seattle, where Mount Rainier rears its 14,408 feet of grandeur, no further word came from it.

From that point on there was complete silence. Presently a state-wide search was begun for the missing craft. Hours later a smudge was noticed high on one of the glaciers, at the 11,000-foot level. Closer inspection revealed bits of metal, wings, and the remains of fire. A ground rescue party set off for the spot.

Backbreaking hours later the searchers reached the spot on Tahoma Glacier where the wreckage had been spotted by the planes. There lay the crumpled transport in scattered bits and broken metal parts. Bloody bulkheads gave mute testimony to the terrific crash against the icy slope in the blinding storm.

The rescue party started a thorough search for bodies — perhaps by a miracle some men still were alive. They looked among the broken parts, into the hollows in the glacier and under crazily tilted wing scraps and cabin wreckage. Then they began to realize that this was no ordinary plane crash. There were no survivors, living or dead, in spite of the evidence that the plane had been carrying men when it crashed. The search continued, but not one body was found — ever. Where did the 32 men go, how did they vanish and why?

# Eskimo Village

STRANGE THINGS HAVE HAPPENED in the long winters of the Far North. But nothing was more baffling than what occurred to an Eskimo village in 1930.

A French-Canadian trapper named Joe LaBelle planned to visit friends at a remote Eskimo village on the shores of Lake Angikuni. As he drew near the village, he noticed that the usual bedlam of the sled dogs was missing. That was odd, he thought, as he approached the little cluster of low sod huts and crude tents spread along the frozen lake shore. Near the first hut he called a greeting, but no answer came.

He lifted the flap of skin over the hut's doorway and peered inside. It was empty, and showed signs of being abandoned in great haste. He went from hut to hut, but all were deserted, and all bore the signs of frantic departure. Pots were still full of food, sewing needles of ivory were left in garments. Even the rifles, so necessary to the Eskimos in this northern wilderness, were abandoned along with food, clothing,

159

and personal belongings of all sorts. More than 30 people – men, women, old folk, and infants – had vanished.

On the shore of the lake Joe LaBelle found three kayaks, including that of the leader of the village, battered by the winds and waves. Seven sled dogs, starved to death, lay by some tree stumps, and an Eskimo grave was open and empty. That was the strangest discovery of all, for opening a grave was unheard of among Eskimos. To add to the mystery, the stones which had covered it had been removed and neatly piled in two groups beside the open grave. Certainly this could not have been the work of animals or vandals.

Joe LaBelle hurried to the nearest town to report his discovery to the Canadian Mounted Police. They returned with him to the deserted village and confirmed his story – all the inhabitants had disappeared into the frozen wasteland without a trace, leaving behind the sled dogs and rifles that would have given them their only chance of survival.

Where did the Eskimos go and why? To this day nobody knows.

# The Spell of the Mirror

IN THE WAR MEMORIAL HOSPITAL at Sault Ste. Marie, Michigan, Jefferey Derosier was close to death. He knew he was critically ill, and so did the three other patients who shared the small ward.

One afternoon Derosier asked the nurse to hand him the small mirror that was on the enamel table beside his bed. The nurse gave him the mirror, which was just a plain piece of silvered glass without a frame or handle.

A moment later he threw it back upon the bedside table and cried hysterically, "I'm dying!" The other patients, watching him, were stunned. He spoke again in a low, dull voice. "You won't be able to pick up that mirror," he said. Then he died.

After his body had been removed, one of the other patients casually tried to pick up the mirror. He couldn't budge it from where it lay on the white table. Baffled, he asked the nurse to pick it up, but she couldn't move it either.

A doctor was called and he too tried to lift the mirror from its place. It would not move. Soon word of the "haunted" mirror spread throughout the hospital, and nurses, interns, and curious patients all tried to move the little mirror from where the dying man had thrown it. No one succeeded. All day the mirror defied all attempts to move it. Even when a nurse tried to pry it loose with an ice pick it remained sealed to the table top.

Then another nurse tried to work her fingernail under the edge of the little piece of glass. As if at that moment the spell was broken, the mirror flew several feet into the air and fell to the floor unbroken. At last it had moved.

Trying to find a reason for the mirror's sticking to the table as long as it had, some of the witnesses attempted to make it stick again. But they couldn't do it. There was no adhesive on the back of the piece of silvered glass and it could now be picked up easily from the dry table top. The surface was wetted in an attempt to make a suction area so that it would stick once more, but the spell was broken, and it no longer remained immovable. Later the mirror was broken, perhaps on purpose, and thrown away. There was never any explanation of the spell cast by Jefferey Derosier's dying words.

# Mule-pen Treasure

THE MULE-PEN TREASURE has provided more frustration than any other lost hoard, because two people have been right on top of it without knowing what was at their feet.

A famous Western badman named Dan Dunham returned from Mexico in 1860, after several months of looting and robbery. With him were a group of his followers and 31 mules loaded with the accumulated loot of the stay below the border. As the desperadoes worked their way along the Nueces River six or seven miles below the Laredo Crossing, following a trail on the south side of the river, they were attacked by a band of Indians.

They seemed to be standing the attackers off successfully, but it looked as if it would be a long battle. Under cover of darkness the outlaws hurriedly threw up a couple of fieldstone stockades for better

163

protection. One pen was for the mules and the other for the men. The mules were herded into the stone pen and the treasure was unloaded from their backs and buried in the ground. Then the mules were turned loose to trample the dirt and remove all signs of digging inside the stone walls.

For several days the fight continued, until the situation became desperate. Dunham finally decided to go to a fort some miles away for help. Although he was seriously injured, he finally reached the fort, but he was in such bad shape that he gave incoherent directions about where the pens and the rest of his party were.

Weeks later, when he was well again, he tried to retrace his steps to the pens. But he never could find them. Eventually he died at the fort, and no one has ever knowingly found the pens or the treasure.

Yet at least two people have been right there, unaware of the significance of the stone pens. In 1866, a cowboy named Pete McNeill spent a stormy night in one of them and wondered what such pens were doing out in that wild country. Later, after hearing the story, he tried in vain to find them again.

More recently a judge from San Antonio camped near them while he was on a hunting trip. Since he had never heard the story either, he did not make a note of their location. Afterward, he too tried unsuccessfully to find them and the treasure they held. Others have told similar stories about being on the spot, but no one has ever returned a second time.

# Swamp Pirate

IN THE SOUTHEASTERN CORNER OF VIRGINIA, extending into North Carolina, there are hundreds of square miles of wet soggy land known as the Dismal Swamp. Few roads cross, and only a few settlements are to be found along the banks of creeks bearing such names as Deep Creek and Chuckattuck.

Many legends and tales of ghosts, phantoms, and unsolved mysteries center around Dismal Swamp, and you could hardly find a more fitting place. The dark waters of the vast swampland are filled with rotting stumps, tall juniper trees and sunken logs. A rank, rotting smell has settled over the area and startling gurgles of swamp gases echo in the stillness of the dark water as bubbles break the surface. The calls of birds and the splash of snakes and turtles are the only other sounds.

Two tales are so often repeated that they may well be true. One is of a girl dressed all in white who paddles a white canoe among the silent stumps and tall trees of the gloomy swamp. Many natives claim to have seen her more than once as they have returned from a hunting or fishing trip in the interior of the swamp. She never answers their calls, they say, but paddles silently past, looking straight ahead, until she and her white canoe are lost to sight among the dripping trees.

The other apparition is even more frightening. During a thunderstorm, when lightning blazes through the trees deep in the swamp, a huge pirate ship appears. It flies the skull and crossbones, and a crew of skeletons man the rusted cannons. As though out of nowhere, the ship comes slipping between the tall trees, while a monstrous pirate stands on the bridge, legs braced and arms folded across his mighty chest.

People say it is the ghost of a notorious pirate called Spade Beard, who once sailed off the coast of Virginia, where his long pointed beard became the symbol for cruelty and terror.

According to those who claim to know, a great storm lifted his ship of terror high across the low coastland and deposited him and his crew in the deep interior of the vast Dismal Swamp. There he is doomed to cruise forever, searching for a way out or a rich prize to plunder.

# Wolves on the Roof

ONE AUTUMN, years ago, when most of New England was still wilderness, a young man and his wife and two children decided to set out to clear some land for a homestead and to build their home. They chose a fairly level piece of land in the woods a few miles from a friend who had already built his cabin. The wife and two small children stayed with the friend while the young man started construction of his cabin.

Finally, the job was almost done. The cabin was built of stout, unchinked logs, and had two small windows set into the frames, one on each side of the stout plank door of split logs. Each day the young husband brought to the cabin another piece of their few belongings so he could save time later on. Soon, the house would be ready for the family.

The impatient wife and youngsters begged to visit their new home, and although the chimney was not yet complete, he finally agreed. Off they went, not knowing that they were embarking on a thrilling and hair-raising adventure.

Since the rough bark roof was already nailed onto the cabin, and only the last few feet of the chimney had to be added, the family decided to spend the night there. But they suddenly realized that they had not brought sufficient food or bedding for the cool fall night. Rather than disappoint the family, the husband said he would go back to his neighbor's house for the things they lacked. He strode off, musket in hand, warning the family not to venture out of the house after dark.

As he had promised to return by dusk, his family did not worry, but set about enjoying their new home. The youngsters frolicked about the yard, climbing the low bank by the corner of the cabin and playing leap frog over the many stumps about the clearing.

Just about sundown, the wife was horrified to notice gray shapes moving stealthily about the edge of the woods nearby. The hair-raising sight immediately called to mind all the things she had previously heard about wolves in that area. She quickly called her children inside and slipped the heavy bar across the door, saying nothing about the elusive shadows so dangerously close.

She soon heard sniffing noises about the cabin, and peering out she saw three large timber wolves hunting for a weak place in the logs. She quickly built a good fire in the fireplace and waited in terror to see what would happen. She did not have to wait long. Suddenly there was a thud on the cabin roof as one of the wolves leaped from the low bank to the rooftop and stood glaring down the chimney hole at the terror-stricken people huddled below. The wife at once heaped more fuel on the fire, and the flames and sparks drove the hungry wolf away snarling. Soon another wolf took his place, then another — their fangs bared and their eyes glowing.

This kept on steadily while the brave wife burned everything within reach. Outside moonlight was already flooding the clearing. Just as the last of the straw from her mattress, the only burnable thing left in the cabin, flared up the chimney, she heard shouts and a shot from outside. Her husband had returned in time to drive the wolves away.

# Real-life Jonah

EVERYONE KNOWS THE STORY OF JONAH and the whale, but how many of you know about James Bartley, an Englishman, who was swallowed by a whale and lived to tell about it?

On August 25, 1891, the whaling vessel *Star of the East* had overtaken a huge school of sperm whales. One of the small boats was lowered, and a crew of harpooners approached a whale which had been wounded with a bomb-lance — a harpoon containing an explosive charge. When the small boat drew near, the great beast suddenly turned and charged, seizing it in its vast jaws and crushing it in two. As the jaws crashed down upon the small boat, the men dove into the water to escape.

The steersman, James Bartley, leaped too close, and the wounded and infuriated animal turned and opened its great mouth as he fell. The jaws closed over him and the whale sank below the surface. The rest of the crew, clinging to the wrecked boat until another dory came for them, thought Bartley was lost for good.

Later in the day a dead whale rose to the surface of the sea, and was dragged to the whaling ship where the crew began to remove the blubber. This took about two days. Then it occurred to one of the men that this might be the whale which had swallowed Bartley. The men decided to cut open the whale's stomach to see.

As they carefully worked through the flesh and membranes, they saw the outline of a human being inside. Quickly they cut away the remaining tissue and there was the missing "Jonah," unconscious but alive. They laid him out on the deck and worked over him to revive him. His entire body had turned purple, but he soon regained consciousness and eventually recovered, the color fading out until his appearance was normal again.

He and the crew who rescued him gave testimony under oath, and the account of the amazing experience was published later in a scientific journal after all the facts had been verified.

James Bartley, in a sworn statement, told of how he felt as the "big-ribbed canopy of light pink and white" descended over him, and the mouth of the great whale closed, how he could feel living fish about him in the stomach of the whale before he lost consciousness from the pressure and heat of the whale's body (the temperature of a whale's body is about 104°), and how, while it was almost impossible to move his limbs, his mind was abnormally clear until he lost consciousness.

# Silver-plated Reef

In 1935, a veteran fisherman named Charlie sailed from his home port of Miami to Key West. He had planned a short trip, but a violent storm kept him at the Key.

After the storm had passed he set out for home in his little sloop. The weather was fine, the breeze steady, and the sun bright. Charlie dozed at the helm as his little craft plowed through the waves on its way back, picking its own course as its skipper slept.

Suddenly the boat ran onto a reef a couple of feet below the surface and heeled over, awakening the sleeping helmsman with a start. The sloop was at a standstill, heeled over at a slight angle on the coral below. Charlie slipped over the side into the waist-deep water to inspect the hull for damage and shove the craft off again into deep water.

As he worked his way around the grounded craft, he became aware that the surface of the small reef was covered with bars or small blocks of dark metal which looked like ingots of some sort. He ducked down and lifted one to the surface. It was heavy and black and appeared to be either pig iron or lead. The top of the reef for several hundred feet was littered with these bars.

Apparently a ship carrying pig iron or lead bars

had been wrecked there and these were all that was left. He hefted the bar in his hand. It weighed about 60 pounds and would make good ballast, so he loaded sixteen of them aboard his sloop. In a short time he worked his boat loose and continued on to Miami.

He thought nothing more of the ballast ingots until about two years later, when his boat was pulled up for an overhaul at a local shipyard. He unloaded the ballast, piled it upon the dock, and sat down next to it while he ate his lunch. Absent-mindedly, he began to pick at the dark crust on one of the bars. Inside he found a shiny metal that looked like lead. Out of curiosity, he took it to a jeweler friend for testing. The bars were not lead at all, but pure silver. He had been sailing around with a small fortune in his ship's bilge for two years.

Ever since then he and others have vainly sought the silver-plated reef somewhere off the Florida Keys. Apparently the storm had uncovered the bars on the shallow reef, but since then another storm had recovered them. Somewhere it still awaits a lucky sailor who may get there between storms when the bars are visible — unless he too is wrecked as was some ancient galleon loaded with treasure a century or so ago.

# Footprints in the Snow

EVERY SO OFTEN a strange event is witnessed by hundreds of intelligent people. Yet not one person can explain it.

There was no denying the footprints in the snow on the morning of February 9, 1855. The odd tracks appeared in several towns in South Devon, England. Residents of Lympstone, Exmouth, Tosham, Dawlish, and Teignmouth all reported the same thing. During the night some weird and uncanny creature had raced in a straight line through these towns, covering a hundred miles and more and leaving behind the tracks nobody could identify.

Each track, about 4 inches in length and 2¾ in width, was exactly 8 inches apart. They were roughly shaped like a hoofprint and were promptly christened "The Devil's Footprints" by all who saw them. Even the conservative *London Times* printed a report of the footprints in the snow.

Going straight across country, the tracks never swerved. They were found upon the top of 14-foot walls and they crossed the roofs of barns and houses, went up and over snow-covered piles of hay and even appeared on the tops of wagons which had been left out all night.

It was as if the creature had leaped up or down,

for the tracks showed no apparent change of pace or speed. In many places it was reported that the snow had been "branded" away or melted from the ground where the "feet" had touched.

Over the hundred-mile course, the distance between the tracks never varied from the regular 8 inches, yet how could anyone or anything travel that far in a single night without varying its stride?

Too many people saw the tracks for it to have been a joke or a local phenomenon. In some instances the prints vanished at the edge of unfrozen ponds or rivers, and appeared again exactly in line on the opposite side, to race away in that straight and mysterious flight across the sleeping countryside. And in all that distance, no one saw it, no one heard it. Only the tracks remained as evidence of the creature's passing.

# The Barbados Vault

WHEN THOROUGHLY RELIABLE PEOPLE encounter ghosts, their stories are difficult to explain away. Such is the case of the Barbados Vault, and what happened there early in the 19th century.

In 1807, the first coffin was placed in the vault. During the next five years the vault was opened twice more and other coffins added. It wasn't until it was opened again late in 1812 that anything strange was noticed.

When the burial party opened the vault and entered to place the last coffin inside, they were horrified to see that several of the huge lead-lined coffins had been tossed about and upset. Yet no one had visited the vault at any time except to place another coffin within. If vandals had entered, what was their motive? There was nothing of value in the dark crypt.

The coffins were straightened and a huge stone slab placed against the entrance to block any further attempts at vandalism. This great slab was so huge and heavy that it took six strong men to hoist it into place against the door.

In spite of this precaution, twice more when the vault was opened the caskets were tossed about. Each time they were put back and the stone slab was replaced.

At last the matter came to the attention of Lord Combermere, then Governor of Barbados. On July 17, 1819, when another coffin was to be placed in the vault, the Governor and other witnesses were present. The Governor had the walls of the vault sounded for secret doors or entrances, but none was found. He then directed that fine sand be spread over the entire floor to reveal any footprints of an intruder. Once this has been done, the only door was sealed and a guard was posted by it to prevent anyone's entering from the outside. This should stop any further vandalism.

Less than a year later, on April 18, 1820, the vault was again opened in the presence of Governor Combermere. Once more the coffins were in complete disorder. The seal had not been broken and there were no footprints found in the sand.

From that time on the vault was left unused, for everyone agreed that it was no place for the departed to spend their eternal rest.

# "Money Lights"
# of South America

PERHAPS SOME OF YOU HAVE SEEN the soft mysterious glow of the phosphorus in an old rotting stump while camping at night, or the flashing lights on the surface of a tropical ocean. These are natural phenomena with which you may be familiar, but did you ever see the unexplainable "money lights" of Mexico and the high Andes of Peru?

These so-called *luces del dinero* are among the legends of the natives. They claim that wherever you see these mysterious lights hovering over the rocky soil or along a jungle trail, there also you will find treasure. They say that the long gold trail from Potosí, Bolivia, to Tucumán, Argentina, where the Spanish used to travel, is pitted with holes, for generations of treasure-hunters have dug where these mysterious lights winked at them.

According to the natives, if you see one of these tall wavering lights, the thing to do is to drive a stake quickly into the ground where it glowed and then go away until daylight. Never try to dig when the light is there, for where the light is there too are *demonios* to attack the careless treasure-seeker.

Some of these "money lights" move along the

178

ground like green pythons, while others stand upright. Some are white, some of a pale greenish color, and some burn with a blue flame. No scientific explanation has ever been found for them.

One man reported that he dug where he saw one such *luz del dinero* to prove that it was all a myth and a mere superstition. Now he's not so sure, for just under the surface of the ground he found a rich gold deposit, now a real mine. A mining engineer said that he almost always found metal ore beneath where the "money lights" flickered.

Another skeptic rented an old Mexican dwelling because an elderly woman had told him that she had often seen the "money light" about the hacienda. The skeptic searched the floors and walls and courtyard but found nothing. But who can say that the old lady had not been right after all? The next tenant also looked for the treasure, and found it. Under the rafters, well hidden in the roof, he found a metal container full of gold doubloons — a small fortune. After that, the light was seen no more.

Those "money lights" that burn with a blue flame sometimes cover the entire area of the treasure buried beneath it. It is peculiar, but these "flames" never burn the grass or vegetation about them, although some of them are reported to flicker and dart like true flames.

# Ocean-born Mary

SOME CONNECTION WITH PIRATES or ghosts or buried treasure is enough to give any house an element of fascination. It's a very unusual house that has a history of all three, and the house near Henniker, New Hampshire, known as the "Ocean-born Mary house" is truly unique.

In 1720 a band of settlers left Ireland and headed for New Hampshire. As their ship, the *Wolf*, approached the Atlantic coast she was fired upon by a sinister-looking vessel bearing down upon her with full sail. The captain of the *Wolf* hauled sail and came to a stop as the other vessel drew nearer.

Immediately a motley crew of pirates boarded the *Wolf* and swarmed over the decks. Their leader, a swarthy buccaneer called Captain Pedro, ordered all the crew and passengers of the *Wolf* to be put to immediate death and the ship plundered and sunk.

He was tearfully informed that a passenger named Elizabeth Fulton had just given birth to a baby girl in her cabin below deck. The pirate's eyes grew soft and he seemed to waver in his plan to murder all aboard. Then he made a deal which was as startling as it was unexpected. If the newborn baby were named after his dead mother, Mary, he would spare everyone. It was quickly agreed and he left at once, sending back some rare silk to be used later for Mary's wedding gown.

From that time on the girl was known as "Ocean-born Mary." When she grew up and married, she wore a gown of the pale-green silk Captain Pedro had provided. The pirate, an old man by this time, went to New Hampshire to end his days, and built the great old house on the hill.

When Ocean-born Mary's husband died, the pirate invited her to join him and share his fortune for as long as he would live. She agreed. One day, she returned from a trip to find him slain with a cutlass. All the servants were gone, and the house was deserted. Mary stayed there until her own death in the early 1800's. The old house built by Pedro in 1760 still stands in a fair state of repair and today it may be visited by arrangement with the present owner and occupant, Mr. Louis Maurice Auguste Roy. It's quite an experience.

When my daughter and I visited it, we were shown through its huge rooms, old hallways, and mysterious alcoves. In one room a huge fireplace has a vast granite hearthstone fitted with an iron ring in the center. This stone, which weighs many tons, covers the last resting place of Captain Pedro, for it is said to be the top of his tomb.

Mr. Roy had told us that he lived in the old house with his mother, and as we were looking at the stone a lady passed silently by the doorway to the outer hall. My daughter and I watched her, but she did not join us or listen to her son repeat the familiar tale once more. We thought no more about it.

We climbed the high railed stairs to see all but one of the upper rooms, and noted the high-crowned floors similar to a ship's deck, for Captain Pedro's carpenters had been more used to building ships than houses. We saw the old piece of Ocean-born Mary's wedding dress and heard all the details of the search for buried treasure around the house.

As we were about to leave, Mr. Roy again mentioned his mother, and we expressed regret that she had not joined us when we saw her in the hall. Mr. Roy looked at us searchingly. "My mother?" he exclaimed. "In the hall? Why, she hasn't been out of bed in months — she's a helpless invalid."

Just who was it we saw pass the hall door as we stood by Captain Pedro's tomb under the hearth of the Ocean-born Mary house on that windswept day?

# Flight into Oblivion

IN THE VAST AREAS OF WILDERNESS throughout the world there are many places where a plane that crashes can be concealed. When a plane is lost over the ocean, there is less chance of finding it, but evidence of the crash is spotted and the plane's fate is at least established. However, once in a while aircraft vanish under such unusual circumstances that we wonder if perhaps some supernatural element did not step in to confound the experts. So it was with the vanished Avengers.

Part of the routine training flights from the Naval Air Station at Fort Lauderdale, Florida, is on a roughly triangular course along a predetermined route. There is nothing unusual or dangerous about it.

On December 5, 1945, five Avenger torpedo bombers (propeller-driven) took off on one such mission — a mission that was to end in tragedy and mystery. The course was to take them 160 miles over the ocean to the east, 40 miles north (toward land), and then back to the base. The pilots and navigators had flown the route many times before. This time was different.

All the planes had the best radio and navigational equipment, each had self-inflating life rafts, and each man wore a life jacket. The planes left after 2 P.M. and were due back in two hours. At 3:45, when they would normally be about ready to ask for landing instructions, the flight leader, after consulting with all five navigators, reported: "Can't be sure where we are. Can't see land." Could *all five* be lost at the same time? Impossible under normal conditions!

Shortly thereafter, the leader turned the command over to another pilot, and 25 minutes later came the last message from the planes: "Still not certain, but believe we are about 225 miles northeast of base. Looks like . . ." And then complete silence. No other radios were heard, nor were there any distress signals.

A vast search was started immediately. One of the planes that took off at once was a giant Martin Mariner flying boat, equipped to land upon rough seas. It was loaded with survival and rescue equipment of all kinds. Base radio advised the Avengers that the Mariner was on its way to lead them home, then called the big flying boat to find out its position and if the men had sighted anything. The Mariner did not answer the call. She too vanished in the same general area without a trace!

The greatest aircraft search in history began. Nearly 250 planes, an escort carrier, many surface ships, and a dozen land search parties scoured the coast for traces of any of the six planes. But the five torpedo planes and the giant flying boat were never spotted. There was not a scrap of wreckage; no floating body, tire, book, or paper; no distress call or rumor. All had flown into oblivion — suddenly, silently, and mysteriously. The report of the Naval Board of Inquiry concluded with: "We are not able to make even a good guess as to what happened." Can you?